Better Homes and Gardens®

SOLAR LIVING

© 1983 by Meredith Corporation, Des Moines, Iowa.
All Rights Reserved. Printed in the United States of America.
First Edition. First Printing.
Library of Congress Catalog Number: 81-70039
ISBN: 0-696-02166-8

BETTER HOMES AND GARDENS® BOOKS

Editor: Gerald M. Knox
Art Director: Ernest Shelton
Managing Editor: David A. Kirchner

Associate Art Directors: Linda Ford Vermie, Neoma Alt West,
Randall Yontz
Copy and Production Editors: Marsha Jahns,
Nancy Nowiszewski, Mary Helen Schiltz, David A. Walsh
Assistant Art Directors: Harijs Priekulis, Tom Wegner
Senior Graphic Designers: Alisann Dixon, Lynda Haupert,
Lyne Neymeyer
Graphic Designers: Mike Burns, Mike Eagleton, Deb Miner,
Stan Sams, D. Greg Thompson, Darla Whipple, Paul Zimmerman

Editor in Chief: Neil Kuehnl
Group Editorial Services Director: Duane L. Gregg

General Manager: Fred Stines
Director of Publishing: Robert B. Nelson
Director of Retail Marketing: Jamie Martin
Director of Direct Marketing: Arthur Heydendael

All About Your House: Solar Living

Project Editor: James A. Hufnagel
Associate Editor: Willa Rosenblatt Speiser
Assistant Editor: Leonore A. Levy
Contributing Senior Writer: Paul Kitzke
Copy and Production Editor: David A. Walsh
Building and Remodeling Editor: Joan McCloskey
Furnishings and Design Editor: Shirley Van Zante
Garden Editor: Douglas A. Jimerson
Money Management and Features Editor: Margaret Daly

Art Director: Linda Ford Vermie
Graphic Designer: Alisann Dixon

Contributing Editor: CarolAnn Shindelar
Contributors: Denise L. Caringer, Emily Freeman, Jim Harrold,
David R. Haupert, Paul Krantz, William L. Nolan
Technical Adviser: Richard Mercer, P.E.

Special thanks to Babs Klein for her valuable contributions
to this book.

INTRODUCTION

It's just about impossible to imagine a world without sunlight. The sun fuels our planet, gives us light and warmth, helps grow our food, and buoys our spirits. With a little encouragement, the sun can do more: It can heat our homes, warm the water we bathe with, even generate electricity.

Solar Living tells about enticing the sun indoors and putting it to work at your house. Notice we said *your house*—the one you now own, not an advanced design you might build some day. Except for one chapter, this book delves into ways to solarize an existing house.

We start off by showing how you can evaluate your home's solar potential, conduct an energy audit, and ready your home to use the sun. Next we explain the basics of collecting, storing, and using solar energy. Then we go into specifics—adding a sunspace, remodeling to open up your house to the sun, picking a domestic hot water system, decorating to make the most of solar energy.

In case you're confused about all the solar processes and systems available today, we explain each as we go, demystifying terms, clearing up points of confusion, and evaluating merits and drawbacks. And if you already have a hammer (or needle and thread) in hand and are eager to get started on a solar project, we show a myriad of possibilities—from solar-efficient window coverings to a whole new house.

Solar Living is one volume in the **ALL ABOUT YOUR HOUSE** library, a comprehensive series designed to give information and engage your imagination about each and every aspect of a modern-day home. Like other books in the series, *Solar Living* includes more than 100 color photographs and dozens of carefully drawn illustrations. Here you'll discover just how appealing solar systems can look and, thanks to the illustrations, how they work. When you've read the ten chapters in this book, we hope you'll say, "Wow, I really learned a lot!"

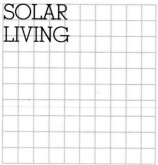

SOLAR
LIVING

CONTENTS

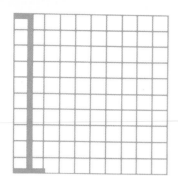

EVALUATING YOUR HOME'S SOLAR POTENTIAL

During the past few years you've probably been hearing quite a bit about solar energy—and perhaps you have read about or visited a few new solar homes. But what about those of us with older, non-solar houses? Can we, too, take advantage of the sun's "free" power? This introductory chapter surveys the jobs nature can do—from heating space and water to generating electricity—and helps you analyze which of them might work at your house. Cross-referencing then guides you to pages or chapters elsewhere in the book that will shed more light on these topics.

Think of the sun as a giant furnace that has been generating energy for billions of years and will continue to produce energy for billions of years to come. Without this furnace our solar system would be cold and lifeless.

The chief beneficiary of the sun furnace is Earth, although it is an insignificant consumer of the sun's vast energy output. Earth intercepts only two-billionths of all solar energy, and half of this our atmosphere absorbs or reflects. Yet the tiny portion that makes it to Earth's surface is 35,000 times more than the total amount of energy used by all the people in the world in one year.

Like rainwater, solar energy can be collected, only a house acts as the bucket. Heating with the sun may seem to be a recent development, but it's an old, old idea—one that dates back to at least the fifth century B.C.

Sunny side up

Ancient Greek architects, like many present-day architects, used *passive* solar heating principles in their designs. A passive solar heating system uses the structure of the building to collect, store, and distribute the sun's heat. Thus, many parts of a building—windows and floors, for example—have both a structural and a solar purpose.

The spacious family room shown *opposite* is a case in point. Two-story-high south-facing windows bring in sunlight. Its heat is absorbed by a solid-masonry floor and a concrete wall at the left of the photo. Later, as the room cools, the walls and floor give off the heat they've retained.

Totally passive systems have no mechanical devices to distribute warmth throughout the house; instead they use the three basic principles of heat transfer: convection, conduction, and radiation. (Chapter 3—"Learn These Solar Basics"—presents a complete discussion of these concepts.)

The active life

When it came to solar heating, ancient Greeks really didn't think actively—active solar heating systems, that is. Active systems use mechanical devices such as solar collectors, water tanks, and pumps to collect, store, and distribute the sun's heat. (Chapter 6—"Selecting Solar Collectors"—surveys the types and uses of active solar systems.) Because of the expensive equipment needed, active solar heating generally is more costly than passive heating, but sometimes the extra cost is justified.

Active and passive solar systems can be either incorporated into a new home (see Chapter 7—"Planning a New Solar Home") or added to an existing house. Start-from-scratch solar houses obviously are more efficient because they are built specifically to suit the site and climate. Still, there are highly efficient ways to convert older houses; which is the best conversion method depends on the size of your house, the direction it faces, the amount of sun your site receives, and the amount you can afford to spend. More about these on the pages to come.

EVALUATING YOUR HOME'S SOLAR POTENTIAL

COULD SUN POWER WORK FOR YOU?

An efficient solar heating system has one obvious major requirement: the sun—and depending on where you live and how your house is sited, getting enough sun could be a problem.

Statistics on the *percentage of possible sun* tell you immediately how much sunshine your area receives. Figures show, for example, that 65 percent of the days in Kansas City are sunny, whereas 45 percent of the days are sunny in Seattle.

For solar heating purposes, the percentage of possible sun during the *winter months* is most important because that's when you need solar heat. The map on page 95 shows the percentage of possible sun for each area of the country in January.

Note that a sunny region may not be one of the warmest areas in the country; the percentage for both Chicago and New Orleans, for example, is the same: 59 percent. However, Chicago is considerably colder than New Orleans, and a solar house in the Windy City needs more solar collecting capability than one in New Orleans. In many Southern cities—including New Orleans—solar homes use only a fraction of the sun available for heating. In those areas, cooling is a much greater concern. Turn to pages 108 and 109 for information about cooling.

How much solar heat does your house need?

The best way to tell how much solar heating you'll need is to determine how cold your area is—which is expressed numerically as degree-days.

Heating degree-days are an indicator of your yearly heating requirement; the higher the number, the more heat you'll need. Chicago has an average yearly total of 6,310 degree-days, whereas New Orleans has only 1,543 degree-days. The map on page 95 shows the approximate yearly degree-days for your area. If you want a specific degree-day reading for your city, call the nearest National Weather Bureau office, or a local meteorologist, weather station, or utility company.

Getting down to specifics

Fortunately, the statistics on sun percentage and heating degree-days show that most locations in the country can benefit from solar heating. When it comes to your specific site, however, other encumbrances may stand in the way. Man-made obstacles, such as high-rise buildings, and natural impediments, such as trees and shrubs, may prevent the sun from shining just where you need it—on the south side of your house. Unless the sun has a clear path to the south side of your home during winter, a solar conversion may be unfeasible. Deciduous trees aren't a problem because they lose their leaves in winter; evergreens, however, may simply cast too much shade. And you can't do much if a neighbor's house or garage blocks the sun.

Most houses enjoy some sunlight, however, and have some potential to make use of solar energy. The challenge is to make the most of the sun power available to you.

HOW SOLAR HEATING WORKS

All solar heating systems are designed to take advantage of the way the sun moves across the sky (or rather, the way the earth moves around the sun, since it's actually the earth, not the sun, that moves). The axis of the earth is slightly tilted, so the earth's revolving around the sun creates longer days in summer and shorter days in winter.

Furthermore, the sun rises and sets in different positions in the sky depending on the season. (See the illustrations, *below.*) On the summer solstice (the first day of summer) the sun rises in the east and sets in the west at its northernmost, or highest, points in the sky. Gradually through summer and fall, the sun rises and sets farther south until it reaches its southernmost, or lowest, points in the sky. This occurs on the winter solstice. Then the sun's path slowly begins its ascent northward once more.

The low path of the sun in winter is the foundation of all passive solar heating systems. Because the sun is low in the sky, it shines directly onto the south face of your house, which is where you should direct your efforts to collect the sun's heat. And in summer, when the sun is directly overhead, you can protect yourself from the sun by using shading devices. A properly designed passive solar system includes methods for both solar collection and control.

EVALUATING YOUR HOME'S SOLAR POTENTIAL

IS YOUR HOME READY TO TAKE ADVANTAGE OF THE SUN?

Tightening up is just what this house needs, according to the thermogram (an infrared photo that shows heat loss) opposite, below. The magenta areas indicate the highest heat loss, followed by red, yellow, blue, and green.

Even if your house is perfectly sited for solar heating, it may not yet be ready for a solar conversion. If your house is poorly insulated and has leaky doors and windows, you'd be wise to tighten it up first before going solar.

A quick way to see whether your home is ready for a solar conversion is to calculate its Home Heating Index (HHI)—a number from 0 to 15 that tells you how energy-efficient your home is; the lower the number the better.

Begin by filling out Table II, *right*. To get the number of degree-days (see pages 9 and 95) for your location, simply call a local weather station.

Calculating your Home Heating Index

(1) Enter the total amount of each type of energy you used last January in Column 1 of the "Calculations" box, *bottom right*. Enter all energy sources, not just those used for heating. (2) In Column 2 enter the appropriate Factor from Table I for each energy source. (3) Multiply Columns 1 and 2; put your answers in Column 3. (4) Add the numbers in Column 3 to get your total BTU usage; enter in the appropriate space. (5) Enter the total degree-days calculated from Table II where indicated. (6) Divide BTU usage by degree-days to get your home's total heating requirement. (7) Enter the total square feet of heated floor area of your house where indicated. (8) Divide your home's heating requirement by the total heated floor space to obtain your Home Heating Index.

If your Index is less than 10, your house is ready for solarization; if 10 or more, concentrate on tightening up your home first (see Chapter 2).

HOME HEATING INDEX

TABLE I: FACTORS

FUELS	Natural Gas (CCF)	LP Gas (gal.)	Fuel Oil (gal.)
Ultra-high-efficiency furnace	90,000	81,000	doesn't apply
High-efficiency furnace	80,000	72,000	98,000
Standard furnace	70,000	63,000	84,000
Pre-1970 or converted furnace	60,000	54,000	70,000

ELECTRICITY (kwh)

Lights, appliances, or resistance heating (without heat pump)	3,400
Same, with heat pump (areas with 500-1,000 January degree-days)	5,000
Same, with heat pump (areas with more than 1,000 January degree-days)	4,000

WOOD (lbs.)*

Airtight stove or furnace	3,500
Non-airtight stove	2,500
Closed fireplace	1,500
Open fireplace	0

*Typical wood weights per cord are: softwoods—2,000 lbs.; mixed or medium woods—3,000 lbs.; hardwoods—4,000 lbs.

COAL (lbs.)

Stoves or furnaces	6,000

KEROSENE (gal.)

Space heaters	135,000

TABLE II: DEGREE-DAY CALCULATIONS

January heating degree-days (reported at 65° F base) for your area		_____
Your average indoor temperature* multiplied by 31	+	_____
	—	2,015
January degree-days for your home (enter *below*)	=	_____

*Average for 24 hours, accounting for any temperature setbacks and average for entire heated floor area (average of warm and cool areas).

HOME HEATING INDEX CALCULATIONS

Energy source	Column 1 Amount used (from records)	×	Column 2 Factor (Table I)	=	Column 3 Energy use (in BTUs)
Electricity _____	kwh ×		_____	=	_____
Natural gas _____	CCF ×		_____	=	_____
LP gas or fuel oil _____	gal. ×		_____	=	_____
Kerosene _____	gal. ×		_____	=	_____
Wood _____	lbs. ×		_____	=	_____
Coal _____	lbs. ×		_____	=	_____

Total BTU usage _____

To help you calculate your Home Heating Index, see directions *at left*.

Total BTU usage _____ ÷ Degree-days _____ = Heating requirement _____

Heating requirement _____ ÷ Heated floor area (sq. ft.) _____ = Home Heating Index _____

HOW CAN YOU BEST USE THE SUN?

Once you determine that your home is ready for a solar conversion, you need to decide the best way to do it. The first step in *solar retrofitting* (converting an existing house for solar heating) is to choose which solar strategies will work in your home. Then evaluate each choice in terms of efficiency (how much solar heat will it collect), cost (how much money it will take to build the system), and aesthetics (what the system will do to the appearance of your house).

A sunspace?

A sunspace is the most popular solar retrofit because sunspaces usually work well with any size or style of home. Besides providing inviting, sun-warmed living space, sunspaces are also very efficient: They usually contribute anywhere from 10 to 50 percent of the heating needs of an average home. But good looks and high efficiency have their price: Sunspace additions can be very costly.

Sunspaces range in size and style from small lean-tos to full-blown additions such as the one shown here. In this 24x12-foot room, the ceiling vaults to the south to capture the sun as late in spring and as early in fall as possible. To protect the space from overheating in summer, the roofline of the addition extends beyond the glass and forms a ridge peak in line with the roof of the house. The sunspace serves as a family room and play area for the kids. Chapter 4, "Adding a Sunspace," shows more sunspace additions.

South-facing windows?

Just as the glass in a sunspace admits solar heat, so do the windows in the south wall of your home. South windows admit solar warmth; east, west, and especially north windows lose much more heat than they gain. Adding windows to the south wall of your home is an inexpensive way to increase its solar-collecting capability. If ordinary windows are impractical, you can add south glazing in other ways. For example, some solar enthusiasts bump out with dormer windows or add clerestories. Chapter 5—"Other Solar Strategies You Can Use"—shows some of these retrofits.

Solar collectors?

Solar collectors can heat your home, heat your water, or do both; and the collectors can use active or passive solar principles. Most of the solar collectors you see on homes today are active units for heating water. In many regions of the country, solar hot water retrofitting is the most cost-effective method available for using solar energy. The appearance of solar collectors on a home is a matter of personal preference, of course, but the proliferation of new systems attests to their popularity. Turn to page 19 to learn whether solar collectors could efficiently heat your home and to page 20 to determine how cost effective a solar hot water system could be for you.

Your own power source?

As solar technology advances, new devices for using the sun will appear on the market. Much of the research in solar energy today centers on the development of new electrical power sources—units that produce power for individual homes or groups of homes. Photovoltaic cells, which convert sunlight into electricity, and wind generators, which convert the wind into electricity, are two devices you may wish to incorporate into your solar retrofit. Turn to pages 22 and 23 to find out more about photovoltaics and to pages 24 and 25 for information about wind energy.

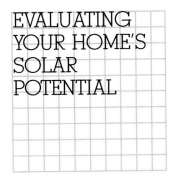
WHERE'S THE BEST PLACE FOR A SUNSPACE?

The steps involved in evaluating your home for a sunspace addition are similar to those for any addition. In the case of a sunspace, however, you'll need to concentrate your efforts on the south side of your home.

Take a look at the south exterior wall: Does your lot have enough room for a sunspace? If your house faces north or south, you may have ample area, but if the house looks east or west, a south-facing addition may end up in your neighbor's yard. If that's the case, you could add active or passive solar collectors (see page 20) or use one of the other solar strategies presented in Chapter 5.

The next step is to make sure local zoning ordinances will allow you to build an addition. In some neighborhoods, for example, setback and other siting requirements may prevent adding on where you would like.

Orientation
For greatest efficiency, your sunspace should face *true south*, or within 20 degrees of true south. The angle can increase to 30 degrees of true south if you can get by with slightly less efficiency.

Don't confuse true south with *magnetic south*, the reading you'll get from a compass. In certain areas of the country, true south varies as much as 20 degrees from magnetic south. Call a local weather ser-

vice or meteorologist to find out the *magnetic declination* for your city. Then if you want your sunspace to get maximum solar gain, pivot its south face accordingly.

Most solar designers, however, design sunspaces to parallel the south wall of the house. That way, the sunspace blends in more easily with existing architectural lines. A sunspace that faces slightly southeast will warm up sooner in the morning and cool off quicker in the late afternoon. Conversely, a southwest-facing sunspace won't warm up as fast in the morning, but will continue to collect solar heat later in the day.

Tying in with the house
Ideally, your sunspace should be next to the rooms you use the most. Any room will benefit from solar heating, of course, but some, such as bedrooms, don't need warmth during the day and can be kept fairly cool at night. So if the ideal spot for your sunspace is next to a less-used room, you may need to devise a method for storing and ducting the heat to other parts of the house (see pages 50 and 51). Or you may prefer to rearrange rooms (convert a bedroom into the family room, for example), move an interior wall, or perhaps expand the living room.

SUNSPACE OPTIONS

How you intend to use a sunspace generally dictates how it should be designed, so determine its exact function at the outset. Will you use your sunspace during the day for extra living space? If so, do you need the room at night, too? Would you like to grow vegetables in your sunspace, or just a few houseplants? Your answers will help you decide exactly what type of sunspace to build. Here are some points to consider:

• A sunspace can be designed for daytime heating only, or for delivering heat both day and night. For evening heating, the key is to incorporate thermal mass to store the day's warmth (see pages 48 and 49) and to install insulating window treatments to prevent the warmth from escaping out the windows at night (see pages 52 and 53). If you want your sunspace to pro-

vide daytime heat only, thermal mass and night insulation are unnecessary; when the sun sets, simply shut off the sunspace.

• An all-glass greenhouse such as the one shown *opposite* will collect solar heat 12 months of the year, not just in the winter. Although that's ideal in climates where a bit of heating is needed year round, in most parts of the country the space would be uninhabitable in summer without a shade covering the roof. That's why most sunspaces have solid roofs, as shown *below*.

• Cultivating a garden in a sunspace is tricky. Most plants can't tolerate temperature extremes, so you'll have to monitor the sunspace's temperature carefully and provide heating when necessary. See Chapter 9—"Growing Food Year Round"—for more about sunspace gardening.

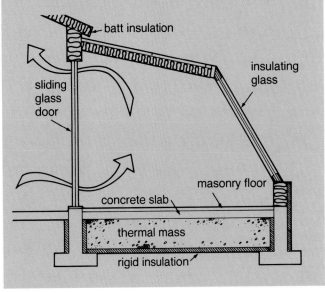

SHOULD YOU
ADD MORE THAN
A SUNSPACE?

Need more room? If so, you can add space *without* adding to your utility bills by building a solar-heated addition. A solar-heated addition is very similar to a sunspace. Both need good access to the south winter sun; but an addition needn't *face* south. As long as one of its walls has proper southern exposure, solar heating will work. This means that a new room added on the east, west, or south side of your home has solar potential; a north addition wouldn't because its south wall would be shaded by the house.

Unlike a sunspace, a solar-heated addition usually heats only itself. If the addition faces south, however, such as the one shown here, or if one of its long walls has southern exposure, the addition could contribute some warmth to other living areas.

A case in point
The 16x25-foot solar family room shown here, for instance, scoops up enough warmth to heat itself and provide 30 percent of the heat needed for the rest of the house. During the day the extra heat is vented to other rooms via existing windows and sliding glass doors. Some heat also is ducted to a rock storage bin in the basement where it's held until needed during the evening.

In the addition itself, warmth is stored in the tile-covered, 5-inch-thick concrete floor and three black 55-gallon drums filled with water (see the photo *at right*). Stored heat from the water drums and masonry floor warms the room as it cools down at the end of the day. (See pages 48 and 49 to learn more about storing heat.)

To prevent overheating in summer, the addition has a deep overhang, shown *above,* that shields the windows from the sun. If the room still gets too warm, doors and casement windows open for ventilation. (Pages 54-57 give more information about keeping solar spaces cool.)

WOULD A COLLECTOR SYSTEM WORK AT YOUR HOUSE?

You've probably noticed more and more glassy rectangles appearing on rooftops these days. Each tells the world that solar energy is working for the family that lives underneath. Depending on the system, the sun might be providing electricity, heating rooms, or—as in most cases to date—heating water.

If you are wondering whether a collector system is feasible for your house, ask yourself these questions.

Does your roof face south?
Of course, a southerly exposure is ideal, but what if your house is sited so one plane of your roof faces east, the other west? First, look at the roof on a detached garage or other outbuilding. If it has the right orientation, a sun collector could work well on it. You would lose a bit of efficiency because of the longer runs of pipes or ducts required, but you might still be able to justify the economics.

The alternative—if you want a rooftop system—is to spend extra dollars customizing your house's roof. You may decide to build a special support rack that spans the ridge, or add a dormerlike structure that angles the collectors in the right direction. Whatever strategy you settle on, by all means get an architect's assistance. Anything the size of a solar collector can have a big effect on the appearance of your house.

Is your roof pitched right?
In addition to facing the collectors south, you also must tilt them at the angle that absorbs maximum sun. As a rule of thumb, a stationary collector tilted at about 5 degrees greater than the latitude of

your site will function quite well for water heating; for space heating, the ideal tilt is the angle of latitude plus 15 degrees. If your roof pitch isn't even close to optimum (usually between 30 and 50 degrees), you may have to resort to a ploy such as the one used on the house shown *opposite*. Here a wedge-shaped bulkhead lifts a bank of collectors toward the sun. Better yet, consider using adjustable racks so you can manually move the collectors several times each year and keep up with changes in the sun's path.

What if your roof won't work?
If for some reason your roof cannot accommodate solar collectors—or you simply can't

get enough of them up there— take a look at your south-facing walls. The home shown *below* boasts both roof- and wall-mounted collectors. The units up top heat water, and the vertical collectors provide space heating.

Does your house have enough space between windows and doors for a few big panels? Does the sun shine directly on the wall most of the day? If not, how about a ground-mounted system? On the plus side is the fact that, assuming the absence of trees and other possible obstacles, you might be able to face and tilt the collectors at optimum angles. (Also, you'd have easy access to the racks whenever you wanted to adjust the angles.) On the negative side,

you may lose efficiency if the collectors are very far from the house.

How about piping and ducts?
Though carving out paths to run piping or ducting usually is the least of your problems— especially if the collectors are mounted at ground level—it's still a point you must consider.

If you want a rooftop installation, you may have to zigzag all the way from the roof to your basement. Thorough insulation is particularly important with pipes or ducts that have long runs or are outside. Advice from the professionals: Plan ahead, and be prepared to make a sacrifice or two. Any tradeoffs, however, are usually well worth the effort.

WOULD A SOLAR HOT WATER SYSTEM MAKE SENSE?

Of all the uses for solar energy, heating water has proven to be the most cost effective for most homeowners. Whether you are one of them depends on at least six factors, four of which only you can evaluate. Here are the points you should think about when considering a solar hot water system.

• *Solar access.* The most important ingredient—the sun—has to be in ample supply at your house. Pages 8 and 9 explain how to judge solar access; pages 18 and 19 tell about angling collectors for maximum efficiency.

• *Roof strength.* Can your roof support the extra burden of two, three, or four collectors? The average panel weighs between 100 and 200 pounds. If you doubt that your roof can withstand the extra poundage, check with an engineer. You may have to beef up the rafters or consider a ground-mounted unit.

• *Cost of fuel.* Are your utility rates so low that alternate forms of energy don't make economic sense? Though utility costs in most cities are high and getting higher, a few communities still boast hard-to-beat rate structures.

• *Cost and efficiency.* The system you select will be a major factor in the numbers game. Of course, the unit that delivers the highest efficiency at the lowest cost will give you the rosiest payback.
Another consideration is the tax credits or other savings you'll be entitled to by adding a solar system. Currently (through 1984), most solar hot water systems qualify for a 40 percent federal income tax credit. This means you can deduct 40 percent of the total cost of the system, up to a maximum deduction of $4,000.

• *Interest rates.* What will it cost to borrow investment capital? What monthly payments can you handle? Do you have savings you can use?

• *Future utility costs.* No one knows how high they'll be. Some experts expect utility bills to quadruple in five years. Others say the growth will be substantially lower. Analysts, however, almost unanimously expect at least a 10 to 15 percent boost annually for some time to come.

How much can solar save?
After you've given some thought to each of these factors, you're ready to make some rough calculations and decide whether a solar hot water system makes financial sense for you. Bear in mind that you should not expect any solar system to supply 100 percent of your hot water

needs. That's because there will be certain times when weather conditions will cause the collectors to produce more heat than you need—or, more likely, less heat. A properly sized unit, however, often can come surprisingly close to producing most of the hot water you'll use.

The chart *below* gets more specific. Indicated in the first column is the average annual percentage of hot water needs that can be supplied by the sun in each of the cities listed. Remember that even though the sun usually can't provide cities in northern climes with a high *percentage* of hot water, a solar heater may still save as much money as a system in a warmer environment because of the cost of fuel.

How much money a solar hot water system will save depends on other factors, too—

the efficiency of the system, how much water you use, even the average temprature of the water entering your heater from city lines or your well. For a quick estimate of the dollars you can expect to save, refer again to the chart. Listed are average dollar savings at each location, based on the cost of fuel used.

For example, if your climate is roughly similar to Chicago and you pay $.08 per kilowatt-hour for electricity, you can save $285 a year by adding a solar hot water system. The dollar amounts are estimates, of course, and are based on a family of four using 80 gallons of 120-degree water per day. The calculations assume a *closed loop* hot water system (see page 88 for a description of this system) that has three single-glazed, 3x7-foot collectors.

ANNUAL SAVINGS FROM A SOLAR HOT WATER SYSTEM

CITY	% SOLAR	NATURAL GAS—$/CCF					ELECTRICITY—$/KWH				
		.40	.50	.60	.70	.80	.05	.06	.07	.08	.09
Atlanta, GA	72	$70	$90	$105	$125	$140	$180	$215	$250	$290	$325
Dallas, TX	80	70	90	110	130	145	185	225	260	300	335
Boston, MA	57	65	80	100	115	130	165	200	230	265	300
Chicago, IL	62	70	90	105	120	140	175	215	250	285	320
Cheyenne, WY	80	90	110	135	155	180	230	275	320	365	410
Fargo, ND	61	75	95	115	130	150	190	230	270	310	345
Kansas City, MO	71	80	95	115	135	150	195	235	275	315	350
Phoenix, AZ	94	85	105	125	150	165	215	260	300	345	390
San Fran., CA	81	80	100	120	140	160	205	245	285	325	365
Seattle, WA	51	60	70	90	100	115	150	180	210	240	270

EVALUATING YOUR HOME'S SOLAR POTENTIAL

COULD THE SUN GENERATE ELECTRICITY AT YOUR HOUSE?

Converting solar energy into electrical energy—a process known as *photovoltaics* (PV for short)—currently makes economic sense for only a few households. With utility rates increasing, however, and the cost of PV hardware coming down, you may find solar-generated electricity a realistic choice in the years to come.

For now, photovoltaics are cost effective only for small homes in remote areas far from utility lines. For these, generators once were the best power sources; today, however, generators cost more to run than they once did.

Stand-alone photovoltaics
For instance, the 1,100-square-foot cottage shown *opposite above* perches high on a California slope about 600 feet from the nearest power line. When the owners asked the local utility company how much it would cost to bring electricity to their house, the answer was $4,000. The owners discovered that a remote or stand-alone PV system was a better choice.

Their system cost $10,000 initially—reduced by a federal tax credit of 40 percent and California's 55 percent credit to an overall cost of $4,000. That's roughly what the owners would have had to pay just to bring in a line so they could buy power from the utility.

Twelve 1x4-foot panels of solar cells, ganged together, catch the sun and convert its energy to direct current. The electricity flows to a dozen powerful batteries that feed some of the power into the household and store the rest. Fully charged, the batteries can store enough electricity to

supply the house for five consecutive cloudy days.

Unlike most PV-equipped houses, this one is wired for both AC and DC current. Lights and small items run directly off the DC batteries; the rest of the appliances get alternating current from an inverter fed by the batteries. Because the inverter wastes about 15 percent of the sun-collected power when it converts DC to AC, the owners use AC only for items that won't run on DC.

Total output is 2,000 watt-hours per day—enough to handle this small cottage (it has a propane refrigerator, range, and water heater), but much less electricity than the average household consumes. That's the problem with stand-alone systems: Unless you're willing to invest in a large bank of batteries, you can't store an adequate reserve of power.

Utility-interactive PV
Utility-interactive photovoltaic systems get around the storage problem by tying into the local power grid. At night, when the systems are not

operating, the owners buy electricity from their utility company; during the day, the utility buys excess electricity from the owners.

Of course, quiet, non-polluting rooftop PV systems seem much more desirable than conventional generating plants—until you look at the price. For example, in the demonstration project pictured *opposite below*, 1,000 square feet of collectors produce 6.9 kilowatts at peak, enough to power the 3,100-square-foot house. Total price tag for the PV system in 1981: about $140,000! That's about $20 per peak watt.

However, some manufacturers already are boasting prices in the $10-per-peak-watt range. As production costs fall even more and suppliers gear up to meet expected increases in consumer demands, prices could drop nearly as rapidly as they did for pocket calculators. Many industry representatives foresee an ultimate price of about $1.60 per watt—a level that's cost-competitive with conventional electricity.

Planning for PV
Clearly, photovoltaics is an idea whose time has not yet arrived, but may well be here soon. This means that if you are considering building a new house or adding to your current home, you might be wise to plan ahead. PV systems have the same needs as other solar collectors, only more so. Tilt angles are critical, and shadows on a PV array can dramatically decrease output. You also need to make sure the PV array will be in direct sun at least between 9 a.m. and 3 p.m.

Thus, you should anticipate the type of mounting system you'll use. The drawings *below* show three possibilities. A *rack system*, generally used on flat roofs or for ground mounting, lets you vary tilt angles. With the *integrated* and *stand-off* styles, the tilt of your array will determine the pitch of your roof. The stand-off version mounts a few inches from a completely finished roof; the integral style, however, *is* your roof, replacing both the sheathing and shingles.

MOUNTING PV COLLECTORS

Rack System
If your roof isn't sloped properly for PV panels, you can mount them (at the optimum tilt for your latitude) on a rack on the ground.

Integrated System
Because an integrally mounted system takes the place of your roof, it must provide mechanical strength and be weathertight.

Stand-Off System
In this system, the PV panels are mounted a few inches above your existing roof and are secured to it with mounting rails.

COULD THE WIND GENERATE ELECTRICITY AT YOUR HOUSE?

If photovoltaics is a new concept, wind energy is an old idea whose time has come around again. At the turn of this century, many American farmers pumped water with windmills, and later added wind generators to produce electricity. Then cheap power came along and wind systems couldn't compete—at least not until recently. Today a good wind-energy system can cost about $2 per watt, a price competitive with many utility costs.

So why don't we see windmills in every backyard? More to the point, would one work in your backyard? The answer lies with your answers to these questions.

• *What's the average wind speed?* The National Weather Service, your local airport, or a nearby weather station can tell you the average wind speed in your area. If it's 10 miles per hour or greater, you have hope. If so, borrow or buy an anemometer (about $175) so you can get a more precise reading. Because the wind generator will go up on a tower of some kind, you'll need to devise a way to take a reading at least 30 feet—and preferably 50 feet—above the ground.

Timing is important, too. If winds are strongest when your electrical usage is heaviest, your chances for a cost-effective system are much greater. (Don't worry about the threat of too much wind; all good wind generators have controls that keep the rotors from spinning too fast.)

• *What about building codes and utility policies?* Local regulations may limit the height of a wind tower or the distances between the tower and boundary lines or roads. Towers may even be outlawed entirely.

Next, inquire about your utility's regulations regarding wind power. Federal laws require utility companies to allow owners of wind generators to tie into the utility's power lines if the wind system meets standard electrical codes; for investment protection, however, it's a good idea to learn whether there will be any red tape or delays in the hookup before you invest several thousand dollars in your own system. Utility companies are also required to buy the excess electricity generated by a wind system, though not necessarily at full retail value.

• *How much will a wind system cost?* You can expect to spend about $2,000 for every kilowatt of energy you want to generate. So, assuming an average household needs a seven- or eight-kilowatt capacity, you're looking at an investment of $14,000 to $16,000 for a generator, inverter, wiring, tower, and installation costs. You can reduce your investment by the 40 percent federal tax credit allowed on the first $10,000 you invest.

Choosing the components

If a wind system is feasible for your home, you'll want to check into the products available. Generators are marketed in a variety of configurations, sizes, and power ranges. Most brands spin on a horizontal axis, as shown in the top drawing in the box *opposite*. This type needs a fin, blade, or other device to keep the unit facing into the wind. A few models—such as the egg-beater type shown in the bottom drawing—operate on a vertical axis and, therefore, can handle winds coming from any direction.

Generally speaking, the larger the rotor the higher its output and price. If you plan to interconnect with a utility company, you don't have to buy a unit big enough to supply the peak amount of electricity your household needs. Instead, you might prefer a smaller system sized to satisfy the *average* amount of electricity you use.

If you're considering a stand-alone system—one independent of the local utility—you'll want to size your system for peak-use capacity. You'll also have to invest in a battery storage bank to even out fluctuations and to store electricity for times when winds are too weak to drive the generator.

Next you'll be shopping for a real attention-getting addition to your site—a gangly contraption that's between 50 and 100 feet tall. The most common type of tower, called a lattice tower because of its latticelike pattern, is used for tall antennas. Other types include telescoping steel tubes and wooden posts, such as the one pictured here. This 75-foot pole, by the way, was installed free of charge by the local utility, as part of its cooperative program to help homeowners reduce peak loads.

WIND BLADES

Horizontal-axis type
The rotor axis of this wind-catching unit is parallel with the ground. Behind the propeller-like blades of these models are fins or some other means of keeping the blades facing into the wind.

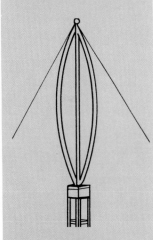

Vertical-axis type
The rotor axis of this Darrieus wind unit (often simply called an egg-beater) is vertical. The egg-beater units readily make use of wind from any direction.

25

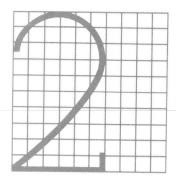

TIGHTENING UP YOUR HOME

With the sun on your side, you can win the battle against rising energy bills. First, however, you have to prepare your home for action by weather-proofing it—tightly—from top to bottom. This chapter describes the strategy and tactics you need to follow: how to do an energy audit, how to plug air leaks, how and where to insulate, and how to ensure your house has adequate ventilation. Taking these steps will make your home more energy efficient and the sun a more effective ally.

Before you can even consider ways to tighten up, you have to know exactly *where* to tighten.

A systematic check of your home's energy efficiency—commonly called an energy audit—will help to pinpoint the places you need to concentrate on. Although most utility companies will do this for a modest fee, you can easily handle the job on your own.

Begin by gearing up for the search. Take along a flashlight, a measuring tape or ruler, a screwdriver, and a candle for detecting air leaks. In addition, carry a pencil and note pad, and jot down the problems you find and the repairs or improvements required.

This page tells you what to look for. Once you've found where the problems are, turn to the pages noted for more information about what's causing a problem and what to do to correct it.

Air check
Inspect those parts of your home where warm air may be escaping and cold air coming in. Check the following:
• Are windows and glass doors double-paned (see pages 28 and 29)?
• Check around all doors and accessible windows. Is caulking in place? If so, poke gently with the screwdriver to make sure the caulk is tight, not loose and crumbly (see pages 30 and 31).
• Test caulking wherever two dissimilar building materials meet—siding and foundation, for example (see pages 30 and 31).
• Check weather stripping of exterior doors and windows by moving a lighted candle around edges. If the flame flickers, air is escaping (see pages 32-34).

• Inspect for caulking or other seals around vents, incoming utility pipes and cables, soil stacks, the chimney, and all other areas where "holes" have been punched through the skin of the house (see pages 34 and 35).

Insulation situation
An uninsulated or under-insulated house needs bundling up before you let the sun shine in. Check these areas:
• Measure the thickness of all accessible insulation—in the attic, for instance—and determine its R-value. Compare that figure with the recommended levels in your area (see pages 36 and 37).
• While you're in the attic, make sure any insulation has a vapor barrier under it; if batt insulation was used, lift it up to see whether it has an attached vapor barrier. And if the space is finished off, look for insulation behind and above the finished area (see page 38).
• To locate insulation in finished attics and exterior walls, remove an electrical switch plate or light fixture and peek in. *(Note well: Turn off the power first.)* If this doesn't work, you may have to make a small hole in a wall to find out how much insulation is present (see page 39).
• Check basement walls for insulation (see page 39).
• If you have a crawl space, look for insulation down there (see page 40).
• Check insulation levels over porches, garages, or other unheated areas (see page 40).
• Look around heating ducts and hot water pipes for insulation (see page 41).
• If the leaks are plugged and the insulation is up to snuff, make sure the house is adequately ventilated (see pages 44 and 45). *(continued)*

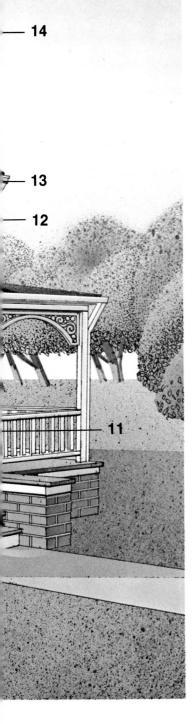

— 14

— 13

— 12

— 11

The house illustrated *at left* may not look just like yours, but it represents a typical home where simple energy-saving features combine to make the indoor environment a more pleasant —and less expensive—place to live year round. More than likely you can incorporate many of the suggestions into your own home.

1. *Gable vents* at both ends of the attic allow superheated summer air, which can get hotter than 140 degrees, to escape. During winter, these small vents let the attic breathe, moving out the moisture that could condense on your insulation and lower its efficiency.

2. An *attic fan* can improve the performance of the gable vents in summer by driving superheated attic air out of the house. At the same time, the fan draws warm air from the living spaces inside the house. This air is, in turn, replaced with cooler outside air pulled in through north-facing windows (usually, it's best to run the fan at night only). One word of caution: On the very muggiest days, don't use the fan. It will bring in humidity with the outside air.

3. All *outside walls* should be insulated. Standard 2x4 stud walls allow enough space for an approximate insulation value of R-13. Consider this a minimum level (see pages 36 and 37). You can attain a higher value here by insulating with rigid foam.

4. *High ceilings* in older homes help keep rooms cool in summer by allowing the heat to rise well above head level. During winter, however, this could be a liability. Add a ceiling fan to gently blow the warmed air back down to the level of the room's occupants.

5. The *thermostat* should be set between 65 and 68 degrees during winter waking hours. (Set it lower for sleeping.) Add a humidifier to make indoor air feel warmer than it actually is. In summer, set your air conditioner thermostat at 80 degrees. As the air conditioner dehumidifies the air, your home will seem to be much cooler.

6. Isolate *unused rooms* from the rest of the house; close their hot-air dampers or shut off their radiators.

7. *Pipes* and *heating ducts* should be well insulated. If not, they will lose a significant amount of energy before warm air or hot water reaches its destination.

8. *Heating* and *cooling systems* should be maintained regularly, and upgraded when replaced. Make certain all fan belts are at the required tension, and oil the motor bearing each spring and fall. Replace dirty filters. In addition, keep the furnace blower in operation constantly. Its motor, which uses little energy, prevents stagnation by generating a continuous air movement inside the house.

9. *Crawl space vents* allow moisture to escape. If moisture were allowed to build up, it would condense in the insulation and greatly lower its heat-holding qualities.

10. *Construction joints* around the house itself should be thoroughly caulked. Any time you add an element to the house, lay a heavy bead of caulking compound to the surface of the lumber joining the new part of the house to the original structure.

11. *Windows* on the north side of the house should be tightly sealed, and double-pane windows or storm windows are mandatory during winter. During summer, take advantage of this shaded side of the house. Admit cool air through these windows by using the attic fan to draw it in and distribute it throughout the house. Keep the south windows closed, at least during the day. The air coming through them will be superheated by the sun.

12. All *doors, windows,* and other *openings* into the house should be tightly caulked. Use latex, acrylic, or silicone compounds, which remain flexible and won't crack as your house settles or the wood in the siding, windows, and door casings contracts and expands with seasonal changes. Doors and windows also should be tightly weather stripped. If they're not, as a temporary measure in winter, apply masking tape or duct tape around the interior of all operable windows to keep out air.

13. *Soffit vents* should be sized to provide the same area of surface openings as gable vents. In other words, they must admit fresh outdoor air as rapidly as gable vents exhaust stale attic air. When adding more attic insulation, be careful not to block gable vent openings.

14. A *fireplace* can be a big energy loser. When in use in winter, it sends enormous amounts of furnace-warmed air up the chimney with the smoke. Even when unused, it constantly lets warm indoor air escape. When you're not using the fireplace, keep the damper closed during winter. If you never use it, consider capping off the chimney.

PLUG ALL AIR LEAKS

Different building materials swell and shrink at different rates, resulting in cracks where siding meets the foundation, for instance, or where flashing comes into contact with roofing. Ignore these cracks, and they'll widen with each passing season, admitting air, water, and insects. Your best weapon against them is a caulking gun charged with the right sealant.

When shopping for caulking compounds, you'll find a variety to choose from. Each caulk is made differently and works best in certain places around your home, but all set up to a chewing-gum consistency that rides out expansion and contraction around them. Use caulk wherever unlike materials meet. The illustration *below* shows typical applications.

Bear in mind that no caulk lasts forever, though some newer types come close. Test old caulk by poking it with a screwdriver or nail. If it cracks, scrape out the brittle material, then recaulk.

As noted, your choices of caulks are numerous: traditional oil- or resin-base compounds, latex, acrylic latex, silicone acrylic latex, silicone, butyl, and polyurethane foam. Which type you select depends largely on the job you want it to do.

Before buying, read product data to learn how to prepare a surface for caulking, which materials the caulk will adhere to, and how long it must cure before you can paint over it. Most caulks shouldn't be applied at temperatures below 50 degrees F or used to fill gaps wider than ¾ inch. Such gaps should be packed first with oil-base rope, oakum, or foam cord, then caulked. The chart *opposite* compares the most commonly available sealants; it will help you choose the kinds that will work best for you.

How to caulk

If you're a novice at using caulk, start in an inconspicuous spot. Some kinds, especially butyl, seem to stick on everything but the surfaces they're supposed to seal; it takes a little practice to find out how hard to squeeze and how fast to move the nozzle for a smooth, unbroken bead. Don't

worry, however; after one or two tubes, you will have the right touch.

An inexpensive half-barrel gun works for most jobs. Its squeeze-action handle forces a plunger against the bottom of a disposable cartridge, pushing the caulk through the nozzle.

To apply caulk, first scrape out old, cracked caulk and peeling paint, then wipe the crevice until it's clean and dry. Insert the tube into the gun, snip off the nozzle's tip, and puncture the inside seal with a nail. Point the gun at a 45-degree angle, pulling it toward you as you work in a slow, steady stroke. Maintain an even pressure on the trigger.

Usually, you're better off applying too much caulk, rather than too little. You can always wipe away the excess and use a putty knife to smooth out inconsistencies.

(continued)

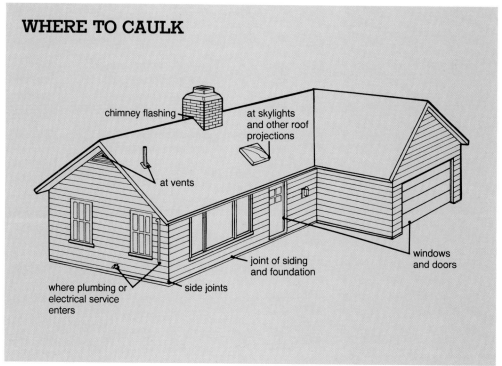

WHERE TO CAULK

chimney flashing

at skylights and other roof projections

at vents

joint of siding and foundation

windows and doors

side joints

where plumbing or electrical service enters

YOUR SEALANT OPTIONS

TYPE	USES	DURABILITY	COST	COMMENTS
Oil- and resin-base compounds	Tube caulk can handle narrow joints, but rope-like oil-base caulk is better for plugging up.	1-5 years	Least expensive ($1.50/tube; $3 for 50 feet of rope)	Although oil-base compounds bond to most surfaces, they dry up, fall out, and need replacing before more expensive caulks. Cover with oil- or latex-base paint.
Latex	Works well on common interior and exterior construction materials when applied in cracks smaller than ¼ inch wide and ¼ inch deep.	2-5 years	Slightly more expensive than oil-base caulks ($1.50-$2/tube)	Highly adhesive, as well as water- and weatherproof, this caulk shrinks over time. Wait two hours before applying latex paint.
Acrylic latex	Seals all types of interior surfaces and is especially good for filling small cracks and tightening up around trim. Use solvent-release acrylic latex on exterior joints.	10-20 years	Moderately expensive ($2-$2.50 per tube)	Acrylic latex is a good, general-purpose sealant that dries fast and can be painted with oil or latex paint two hours after application.
Silicone acrylic latex	Works on wood, masonry, and other interior or exterior building materials.	25 years	Moderately expensive ($3/tube)	A super-elastic sealant, silicone acrylic latex provides long-lasting protection against air and water seepage. You can paint over it with oil or latex paint just 30 minutes after applying.
Silicone	Effective for sealing around tubs, masonry, glazing, outdoor fixtures, and solar collectors.	10 years	Expensive ($5-$7 per tube)	This is an excellent waterproof sealant that works for most surfaces. Save it for small jobs requiring exceptional adhesion and long-lasting elasticity. Silicone sets up quickly but resists painting.
Butyl-rubber-base compounds	Good exterior caulk for metal joints where little or no movement occurs. Use to seal seams in gutters; around roof flashings, storm windows, air conditioners; and between metal and masonry.	20 years	Moderately expensive ($1.50-$2/tube)	Butyl remains flexible after the skin forms over it. Wait for 7 days before painting, and avoid using it in climates where the temperature drops below −10 degrees F.
Polyurethane (expanding) foam	Ideal for sealing cracks between the sill and foundation, between door or window jambs and headers, and wherever air leaks occur. Insulates, too.	20 years	Expensive ($4-$5 per 14-ounce can)	This sealant cures best where the humidity is high. To allow for foam expansion, fill only about half the cavity. Trim off the excess, and cover with caulk or paint or both to shield the foam from damaging sunlight.

PLUG ALL
AIR LEAKS

(continued)

SELECTING WEATHER STRIPPING

MATERIAL	INSTALLATION	COST	DURABILITY
ROLLED VINYL AND FELT	Tubular in cross-section (see the drawing *opposite, lower center left*), these have a flange you staple to door or window stops. Cut with scissors or snips. Align so the strips' bulbous edges project slightly for a compression fit. Rolled vinyl and felt are visible when installed.	Moderately expensive	Good
SPRING METAL	Thin metal strips, folded along their length; spring metal expands to fill gaps along window or door edges, as shown *opposite, lower far left*. Cut the metal with snips, then tack into place. For a tighter fit, gently pry along the strips' lengths. Makes a tight, invisible seal.	Moderately expensive	Excellent
SELF-ADHESIVE FOAM	Very easy. Snip it with scissors, peel off the paper backing, and press the strip into place.	Inexpensive	Only fair; foam breaks down, and friction can pull strip loose. Foam weather stripping works best in compression-only situations, such as the one illustrated *opposite, lower center right*.
INTERLOCKING METAL STRIPS	Several different configurations—some are exposed (such as the one illustrated *opposite, lower far right*); others disappear when you close the door or window. All are fairly difficult to install because you must align them exactly. Interlocking metal strips work only on doors and casement windows.	Expensive	Excellent, but some types for outdoor use are subject to damage.
DOOR SHOES, SWEEPS, AND THRESHOLDS	Some mount on the bottom of the door; others replace an existing threshold. Installation can be tricky for some types, but easy for others. For illustrations of door sweeps, shoes, and thresholds, see the inset drawings on page 34.	Moderately expensive to expensive	Fair to excellent

DOUBLE-HUNG WINDOW

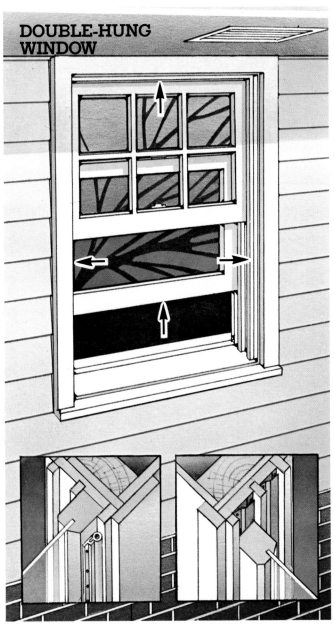

CASEMENT WINDOW

To test for air gaps in your home, choose a cool, windy day, and pass your hand around any openable part. If you feel a breeze, you've found an air gap that needs sealing.

Note that some types of heat loss, such as radiation through single-pane windows, seem to produce a draft, but actually don't. If you have doubts about which kind you're dealing with, test for leaks using a lighted candle (see page 26). Or cover the window with plastic, and watch for movement.

Measure the dimensions of the edges where the leaks occur. To determine how much weather stripping you need, total the measurements, and add about 10 percent to allow for waste.

Note how each window and door fits into its frame so you can select the best weather stripping for a tight seal.

The chart *opposite* is a handy guide to the kinds of weather stripping most commonly available. Once you've bought the type you need, look over the illustrations *above* and on the following page; they show precisely how weather stripping protects double-hung and casement windows, as well as exterior doors.

(continued)

PLUG ALL
AIR LEAKS
(continued)

WEATHER-STRIPPING
EXTERIOR DOORS

self-adhesive foam

rolled vinyl

spring metal

sweep

bulb threshold

Air leaks sometimes result from more than just a loose fit. A badly rotted sill or warped sash may be another culprit. Or, dried, broken glazing compound around glass panes on the outside of a window can provide an exit for warmed house air. In these cases, fix the faulty elements first, then weather-strip.

One of your house's chief energy wasters could be its exterior doors. A poorly weather-stripped exterior door can leak up to twice as much air as a window in the same condition. Couple this with the fact that most doors are used far more often than windows, and you can see why their seals merit careful attention.

Many doors often have crimped, flattened, or missing weather stripping at the top and sides. A door's bottom edge can pose additional problems. Its threshold—sometimes called a saddle—has to withstand a lot of wear. Plus, any seal you attach to the door itself must clear carpeting or unevenness on the floor within the arc the door traverses. Devices such as those shown *at left* (and described in the chart on page 32) solve these difficulties, some better than others.

For some problems, however, other solutions may be necessary. For example, you may need to replace worn-out thresholds. Or, if your door is warped or has a heat-wasting hollow core, the best idea may be to remove it and install a solid- or foam-core door.

To correct an out-of-square frame, take off the door, remove the nails holding the trim and jamb in place, and reset the frame. Finish the work by replacing the parts and caulking around the exterior door trim.

Finally, remember: Doors that open directly to the outside aren't the only ones that require weather stripping. Any interior doors that open to an attic, garage, basement, or other unheated space should receive the same attention.

Other leakers

Caulking to seal outside cracks and weather-stripping windows and doors will take care of most major leaks. But other parts of your house may be leakers, too.

Do you know, for instance, that baseboard molding on exterior walls can serve as an inroad for cold air? Take a moment to feel along the baseboard. If you detect a draft, pry the baseboard off to find where the air is coming from. You'll more than likely discover crevices here you didn't know existed.

Further, if drywall tape in corners has cracked or pulled away from the wall, you can bet energy is wasted here, too. Reseal these areas by replacing the tape and covering it with drywall compound.

In addition, feel around the exposed ductwork joints in your basement when the furnace blower is on. If you notice heated air oozing out, wrap duct tape around the leaky joints. Check, too, around your home's dryer, range hood, and bathroom vents. If their magnet- or gravity-activated dampers don't close properly, they're losing a lot of heat. You'll have to repair the dampers. With clothes dryer vents, you can do more than this by bringing air heated in the dryer back into the house. To do it, buy a hot-air diverter made especially for the job. (For more about plugging leaks, see the box *at right*.)

STOPPING THREE MAJOR LEAKS

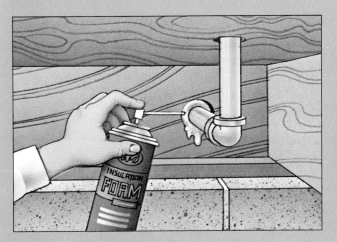

To prevent cold air from entering and heat from leaving, block air passages around electrical service and plumbing lines that run into the house. For especially large holes, first insert oil-base rope, foam rope, or oakum, then caulk. Or, do both jobs at once by squirting the cavity just under halfway up with expanding, insulating foam, as shown here.

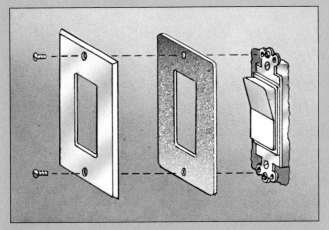

Though often overlooked, electrical outlets and switches are big energy wasters. Because they poke through wall insulation, they serve as points of least resistance for cold air to come into and warm air to exit your house. Correct this problem by installing inexpensive foam seals such as those shown *at left*.

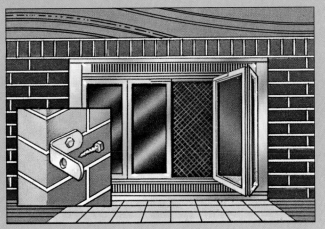

A fireplace can roar out of control, routing many costly BTUs of warmed house air right up the chimney. Do something simple: Keep the damper closed when you're not using the fireplace, and you'll keep a few of those otherwise-lost BTUs. Save even more by installing glass doors within or over the fireplace opening, as shown *at left*.

INSULATE

If your home lacks insulation entirely, you're probably well aware of the huge amount of heat exiting through its exterior surfaces. Wrapping them up in insulation can cut this energy loss—and, as a result, your heating and cooling bills—by as much as 50 percent or more. Most existing houses, however, are really just *under-insulated,* with some meager protection in important spots and none at all in others.

To figure how much insulation is enough for your home, you first need to know what an R-value is. Simply, an R-value is a measurement of how well a material resists the flow of heat. The higher the R-value, the greater the resistance and the warmer your home will be in winter. Nearly every building material —wood, masonry, fiberboard sheathing, even glass—offers some resistance to heat transfer. However, their differences vary only slightly from house to house, so for your purposes, you need only determine what type of insulation you have and how much of it.

You can do that by measuring the thickness of your insulation in inches and then referring to the chart *opposite.* It shows how different kinds of insulation have different R-values per inch. It also describes where materials work best and how to install them. Your choices are many and varied. Here's a short analysis of the major kinds.

• *Batts* generally consist of fluffy fiber glass or rock wool of various thicknesses in sections 15 to 23 inches wide (to fit joist and stud spacings) and 4 to 8 feet long. They are moisture- and fire-resistant, and come either with or without an attached vapor barrier.

• *Blankets*—also fiber glass or rock wool and sized to fit between framing—come in continuous rolls you cut. This means less waste, but also makes blankets more difficult to handle.

• *Loose-fill* insulation can be poured or blown into cavities. The most common are fire-retardant cellulose fiber, vermiculite, perlite, fiber glass, and rock wool. Loose-fill insulation can be installed in finished wall and floor cavities.

• *Foam* (urethane) works well in insulating finished walls, floors, and ceilings from the outside. Foam has a higher R-value than blown-in insulation, but it's also more costly, and often shrinks after a time.

• *Rigid* insulation consists of boards made of molded or extruded polystyrene, polyurethane, or polyisocyanurate. Polyurethane has a very high R-value, but along with polystyrene, it's highly combustible and must be covered with at least a ½-inch thickness of drywall to protect against fire.

After you've identified and measured your home's insulation, tabulate the total R-value for your attic, walls, and floors. Using the map shown *below,* compare these figures with those recommended for your part of the country.

If you need to add insulation, you'll have to decide whether you want to do the work yourself or have an insulation contractor do it. Either way, your house—and your pocketbook—will be able to handle winter's worst weather.

(continued)

R-VALUE ZONES

Zone	Ceiling	Wall	Floor
E	R-38	R-19	R-22
D	R-33	R-19	R-22
C	R-30	R-19	R-19
B	R-26	R-19	R-13
A	R-26	R-13	R-11
F	R-19	R-11	R-11

Based on average heating and cooling needs, the map shows minimum amounts of insulation recommended for walls, ceilings, and floors in each region of the country.

COMPARING INSULATION MATERIALS

TYPE	R-VALUE*	USES	INSTALLATION
BATTS			
Fiber glass	3.0	Unfinished attic floors, rafters, crawl spaces, walls, ceilings.	Lay them in place; friction-fit between framing members, or staple.
Rock wool	3.0		
BLANKETS			
Fiber glass	3.1	Unfinished floors, rafters, crawl spaces, walls, ceilings.	These usually have flanges that staple to framing.
Rock wool	3.0		
LOOSE-FILL: POURED			
Fiber glass	3.1-3.3	Unfinished attic floors, especially those with irregular joist spacing or lots of obstructions. You can also use them to fill walls and other cavities.	Very easy if you can get at the cavity. Just pour to the right depth, making sure you fill every cranny.
Rock wool	3.0-3.3		
Cellulose	2.8-3.7		
Vermiculite	2.0-2.6		
Perlite	2.5-4.0		
LOOSE-FILL: BLOWN			
Cellulose	3.1-4.0	Finished ceilings, walls, floors, and other closed cavities.	You can rent machinery for this fairly tricky operation. Better yet, hire a contractor.
Fiber glass	2.8-3.8		
Rock wool	2.8-3.8		
FOAM			
Urethane	6.2	Finished ceilings, walls, floors, and other closed cavities.	Professionals inject this into cavities, then it hardens. Make sure the contractor is certified. Works as an effective vapor barrier.
RIGID			
Polystyrene	4.0-5.4	Roofs, ceilings, walls, foundations, basement walls, and other places you might need thin material with a high R-value.	Use adhesive to install panels, or friction-fit. Because the first two are combustible, they must be faced with drywall.
Polyurethane	6.7-8.0		
Polyisocyanurate	8.0		

VAPOR BARRIERS: Because homes generate (on the average) 18 gallons of water vapor per week, protect your insulation from moisture using a 2-mil or greater polyethylene vapor barrier. Note that some insulation comes with a vapor barrier of kraft paper or foil.

*per inch thickness

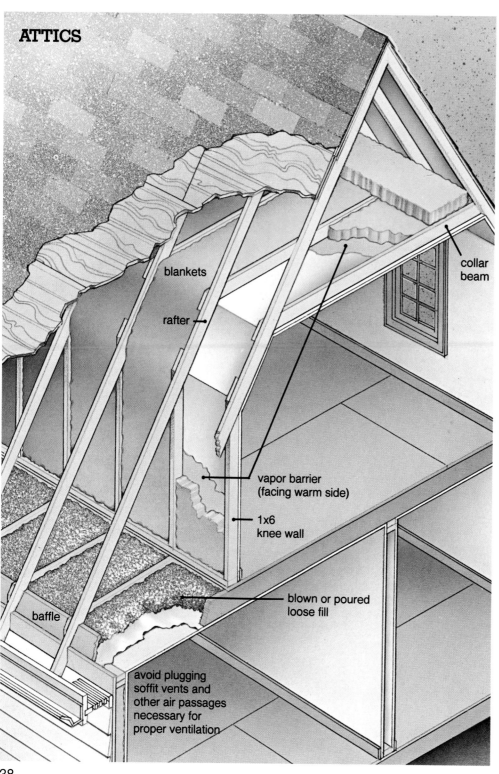

ATTICS

blankets

rafter

collar beam

vapor barrier (facing warm side)

1x6 knee wall

blown or poured loose fill

baffle

avoid plugging soffit vents and other air passages necessary for proper ventilation

An uninsulated or poorly insulated attic squanders energy by sending heat right through the roof in cold weather, and by serving as an enormous solar collector on hot, sunny days. Raise the R-value here, and you can reduce your heating and cooling costs considerably.

Exactly how you go about insulating your attic depends on how you're using or planning to use the area. If it'll never be anything more than storage space, insulate only the floor. If, however, you expect to finish it off, construct a room within a room by adding collar beams overhead and knee walls between the rafters and floor joists. Then insulate around these, as shown *at left*.

Either way, first look for roof leaks that may damage insulation, check to ensure you have adequate ventilation, and consider whether to add an attic or whole-house fan to cut summer heat buildup even more (see pages 44 and 45).

If your attic has a floor, you'll have to pull up sections of it and work the insulation underneath, or hire a contractor to blow in loose-fill. With unfinished floors, put down some planks to keep from stepping through the ceiling below.

For the insulation itself, you can get batts, blankets, rigid boards, or loose-fill. If you already have a vapor barrier, use unfaced materials, or slash the facing so moisture can't become trapped between two barriers. Note, too, that it's important you don't cover recessed light fixtures or exhaust fans; this could cause a fire.

Caution: Some materials, such as fiber glass and mineral wool, are harmful to lungs and skin, so be sure to wear a painter's mask, gloves, and a long-sleeve shirt if you plan to work with either type.

WALLS

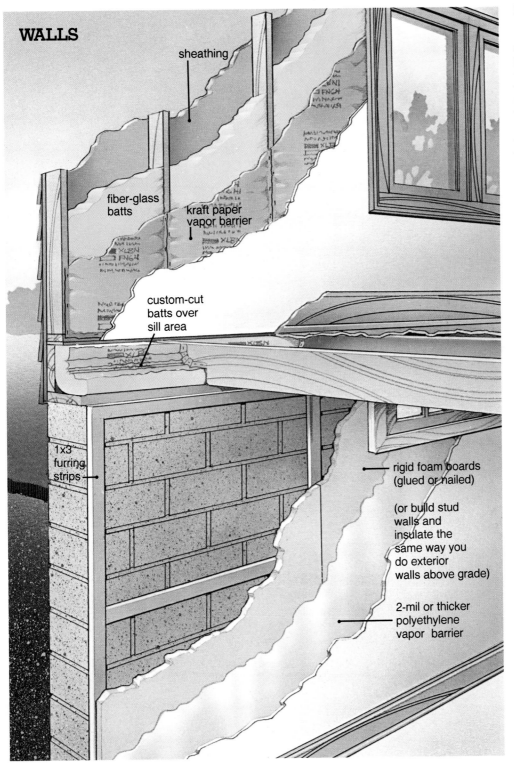

sheathing

fiber-glass
batts

kraft paper
vapor barrier

custom-cut
batts over
sill area

1x3
furring
strips

rigid foam boards
(glued or nailed)

(or build stud
walls and
insulate the
same way you
do exterior
walls above grade)

2-mil or thicker
polyethylene
vapor barrier

The best time to insulate exterior walls is during construction. If you're adding a room, for instance, fit batts or blankets snugly between studs as shown *at left*. If they're backed with a vapor barrier, staple the flanges to the edges of the studs at 8-inch intervals. With unbacked fiber glass or rock wool, friction-fit tailored pieces between studs, then staple on sheets of polyethylene to make a vapor barrier. For added R-value, consider nailing or gluing rigid-foam panels to the outside of your stud walls before the siding goes up. Also, make sure to stuff all cracks around windows, doors, and other areas with insulation.

If your walls already are finished, don't assume you can't do anything about them. Be aware, however, that insulating existing walls is neither easy nor inexpensive; it usually means hiring an insulation contractor with the right equipment and know-how.

You have two kinds of insulation to choose from: loose-fill and foam. Each is installed similarly. A contractor bores holes into the wall cavities, from either the inside or the outside of the house; sizes the space to be insulated; then fills the cavity using a nozzle and hose connected to a pump and holding tank.

If you're thinking about finishing off a chilly basement, you definitely need adequate insulation. Install it in one of two ways. Use rigid boards nailed or glued to furring strips, as shown in the illustration *at left, below,* or fit soft batts or blankets of insulation between newly constructed stud walls. Which you choose depends on where you live, and how much space you're willing to give up for insulation.
(continued)

INSULATE

(continued)

Unheated crawl spaces need to be bundled up tightly, also. Here, you have two options: Drape batts or blankets around the space's perimeter walls, as shown *at upper right,* or suspend material between or from floor joists, as shown *at lower right.*

Draping the walls generally gives better results (and warmer floors) because the crawl space becomes a sealed air chamber and adds further insulation value. With some homes, however, you have no choice but to insulate the floor between the joists.

Wrapping up a crawl space is a dirty but not difficult chore—providing you really do have space to crawl around down there. You'll need *unfaced* batts or blankets, enough 4- to 6-mil polyethylene to cover the ground underneath, and some 1x2s and nails to secure the insulation to the boxing. Also gather up a few bricks or rocks to hold down the polyethylene and insulation.

Floors over unheated areas require bundling up, too. Exactly how you handle these major heat-eaters depends on the situation underneath.

If the joists are covered, your best bet is to have a contractor blow in loose-fill. With open joists, install batts, blankets, or rigid boards. Blankets or—better yet—batts make sense if spaces between the joists aren't chopped up with lots of pipes, wiring, ducts, or bridging. Suspend these between floor joists, using wire mesh or 1x2s.

Boards let you drop below many of these obstacles, but check building codes before choosing this option. You'll probably have to use a noncombustible material to face foam boards.

CRAWL SPACES

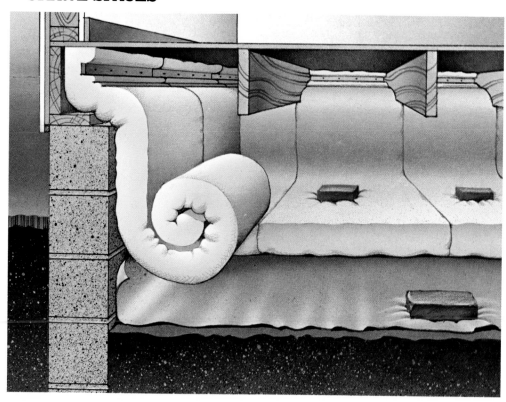

FLOORS

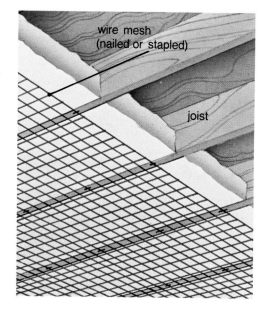

wire mesh (nailed or stapled)

joist

SUPPLY DUCTS AND HOT WATER PIPES

Believe it or not, failure to insulate the pipes and ducts in your home—especially any that run through an unheated area—can result in a 10 or even 20 percent energy loss. Insulate these, as shown *at right*, and you can prevent most of this waste.

To begin with, uninsulated hot water pipes allow heat to escape, which in turn forces the water heater to work much harder. Wrap them with custom-cut sleeves of insulating foam. At pipe junctions, wrap all uncovered areas with spongy insulation tape: Simply peel off the backing and wrap the tape around the joint as you would a bandage around your finger. Wrapping *cold* water lines won't save energy, but it will eliminate sweating and dripping.

For ducts that run through unheated spaces, such as an unheated basement, you have a choice. If you're planning to use the space as a primary living area, you may be counting on heat loss to keep things warm down there. In this situation, you might be better off to insulate the walls (see page 39) and forget about the ducts.

If, on the other hand, your basement gets only occasional use, consider installing a couple of new basement registers and insulating both the ducts and the floor above.

To insulate ducts, protect those running between joists with 1- or 2-inch ductwork blankets stapled to the subfloor above, their vapor barrier facing to the outside. For ductwork running below and across joists, wrap all four sides (and any exposed ends) with ductwork blankets. In each case, first seal all joints with duct tape. *(continued)*

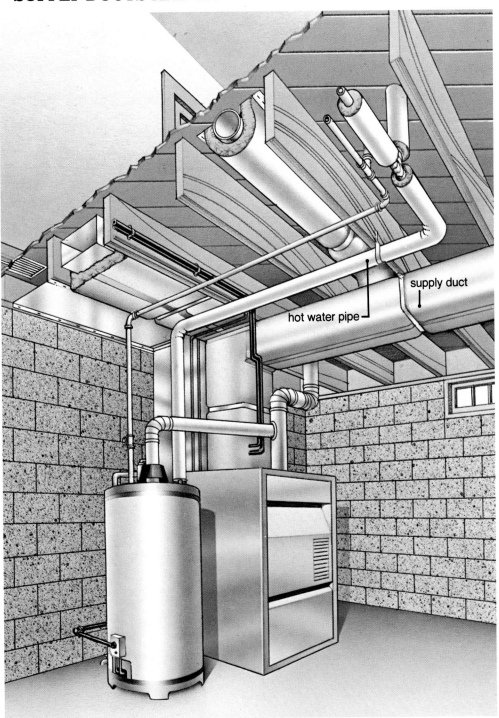

supply duct

hot water pipe

CONSIDER
SUPERINSULATING

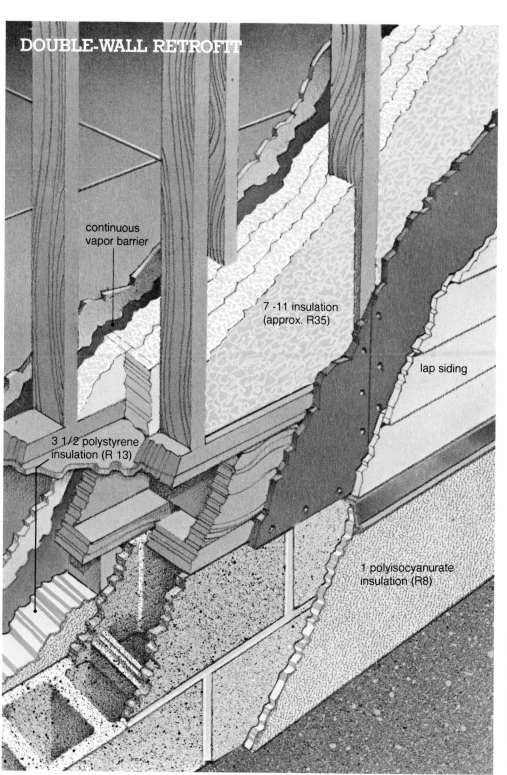

DOUBLE-WALL RETROFIT

continuous
vapor barrier

7 -11 insulation
(approx. R35)

lap siding

3 1/2 polystyrene
insulation (R 13)

1 polyisocyanurate
insulation (R8)

Superinsulating incorporates large quantities of insulation and an airtight vapor barrier; in effect, it wraps up a home and seals out the weather. It can include air-lock entries, triple-glazing on north-facing windows, and an air-to-air heat exchanger for ventilation.

Although it's less costly and easier to superinsulate a house during construction, you can do it anytime. What you must decide is whether the changes will be cost effective. In well-insulated homes it may take many years to recoup your investment. However, under-insulated houses are good candidates for superinsulation.

If you're unsure about the cost of superinsulating your home, ask an architect or building contractor for advice. As a less-expensive alternative, ask your local utility to conduct an energy audit of your house (or do your own; see pages 26-29). With the audit information, calculate the cost of tightening up and, at the same time, figure the payback period—the number of years needed to recover your initial investment. You may find that simple weather stripping and caulking will be the best ways to save money.

Which approach is best?
If superinsulating *is* the answer for your house, you can do it in one of two ways, using the single-wall method or the double-wall method. With the single-wall option, you add insulation to the exterior of your home; the double-wall method calls for building another set of perimeter stud walls in from existing walls. Generally, unless your house has a brick or stone facade, it's easier to add insulation to the outside.

Most of us are familiar with what insulating does for a home. Super-insulating does more of the same—allowing you to conserve almost every bit of indoor energy and to recycle it repeatedly.

• *Double-wall retrofits.* As you can see in the illustration *opposite,* a second perimeter wall set in a few inches from the existing one (distance depends on the insulation used) allows you to nearly triple the R-value. A continuous vapor barrier, sealed carefully, effectively blocks the passage of air into or out of the house. Note, also, that foam insulation outside and in beefs up the R-value of the foundation walls.

Of course, doing all this means making other changes, as well. You'll need to relocate air-duct openings and electrical outlets to the new wall. Plus, the new double walls will require that you frame-out windows and doors to accommodate the increased thickness.

Before beginning work on the walls, turn your attention upward. Install additional insulation in the attic to a total of 16 inches (that's about R-50). Make sure to caulk and weather-strip all openings leading into the house's living areas.

• *Single-wall retrofits.* The object of this approach is the same as with the double-wall option—only the techniques differ. Here, you add extra insulation to the exterior. To build a wall like the one shown *at right,* first remove the siding and nail up 4-inch-thick panels of rigid foam. These panels should extend from the eaves to at least 4 feet below grade.

Next, glue plastic mesh to the foam, followed by a ⅛-inch layer of epoxy/cement stucco. Trowel it on over the mesh to form a continuous, fine-textured surface.

As before, you'll have to extend window and door jambs, insulate the attic to R-50, and caulk and weather-strip all openings. Also, if the wall doesn't have a vapor barrier, apply vapor-barrier paint to the walls and ceiling.

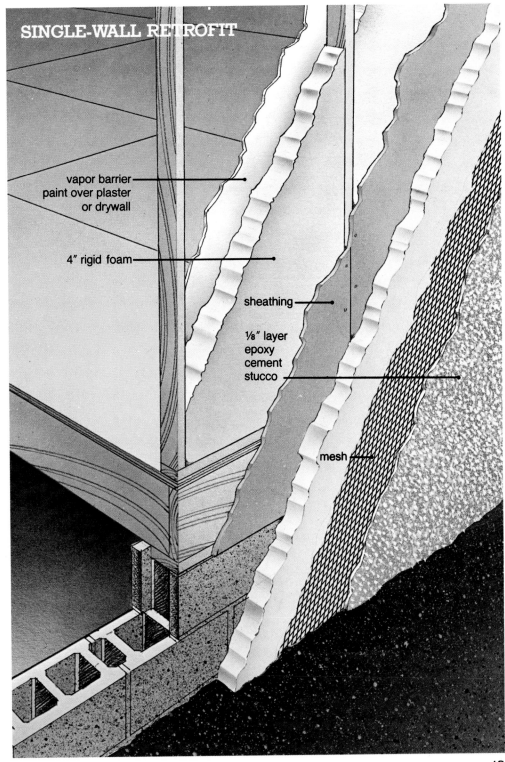

SINGLE-WALL RETROFIT

vapor barrier paint over plaster or drywall

4″ rigid foam

sheathing

⅛″ layer epoxy cement stucco

mesh

IMPROVE VENTILATION

Every house needs a breath of fresh air—at the right time and in the right places. Once you've successfully sealed the heated areas of your home, you will probably have to provide extra ventilation in spots such as unheated attics or crawl spaces. Certain other areas and equipment also require venting.

Builders and architects know the importance of adequate ventilation. That's why most homes have soffit vents and roof louvers or gable vents to prevent heat buildup during summer and moisture accumulation during winter. Most homes also have exhaust fans in the kitchen and in windowless bathrooms to help remove unwanted vapors and odors. And if a home has a crawl space rather than a basement, it typically has at least two vents near opposite corners.

Today, however, with increasingly higher energy costs and with new construction methods and materials that result in tighter houses, ventilation is more important than ever before. Not only are well-ventilated houses more comfortable at cooler temperatures in winter and at warmer ones in summer, but they're more environmentally acceptable, as well. In fact, scientists have begun to show that in certain instances, improper ventilation can lead to visual and nasal discomfort and other more serious ailments.

Fortunately, for most of us the major concerns are comfort and energy savings. Using a combination of the devices shown *below,* you should be able to create enough ventilation to give you both.

To help determine your needs, read the chart *opposite*. It pinpoints ways to bring in fresh air and expel stale or humid air. For example, did you know that you can save a lot on your air-conditioning bill (and greatly reduce frost build-up on your attic rafters and sheathing) by installing a wind-activated turbine or electric attic fan on the roof? Or, that to exhaust warm air quickly from your home during the summer months, a whole-house fan is tops?

The chart lays out ways to supply fresh air for combustion to your home's furnace or boiler without using heated air from the house. Should you ever need to add an exhaust fan in a new bath or remodeled kitchen, you can find help in the chart for that, too.

(The *CFM* ratings in the chart describe cubic feet of air moved per minute. They allow you to choose a unit, rated in increments of 10 CFM, according to the space it must handle and the speed at which it will exchange air.)

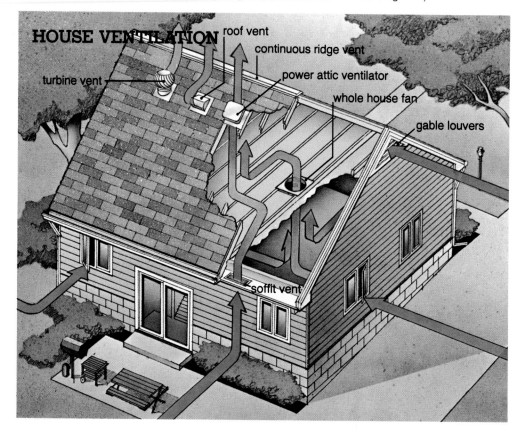

HOUSE VENTILATION
roof vent
continuous ridge vent
turbine vent
power attic ventilator
whole house fan
gable louvers
soffit vent

BRINGING IN AND EXHAUSTING AIR

LOCATION	INSTALLATION POINTERS	REQUIRED CFM RATING
ATTIC **Soffit louvers** **Roof vents**	Space soffit louvers at regular intervals along the overhang, making sure, at the same time, that insulation isn't blocking the flow of air into the attic. Install roof vents high on the side of the roof so they're not visible from the street. You can substitute continuous ridge vents or triangular gable vents for the roof vents.	If the ceiling insulation has a vapor barrier below it, allow 1 square foot for each 300 square feet of attic space. If not, allow 1 square foot for each 150 square feet.
Wind-powered fan **Electric-powered fan** **Whole-house fan**	Install wind- and electric-powered fans on the back side of the roof, near the ridge, but not higher than the roof itself. You can also mount electric-powered fans on a wall or gable end. Mount turbine fans an equal distance in from each end of the roof. If possible, install whole-house fans in a central hallway. You'll also need a power attic fan to exhaust air coming into the attic.	For electric fans, multiply the square footage of the attic by 0.7 to determine the CFM rating. If your roof is dark in color, add 15 percent to this figure. If you're using turbine-powered fans, you'll need two, unless your attic has more than 1,200 square feet, in which case you'll need three. To size whole-house fans correctly, multiply the square footage of the living area by 3 for the minimum CFM rating.
BATHROOM **Bathroom fan**	Following the manufacturer's instructions, install an exhaust fan in the ceiling, near the center of the bathroom.	For the CFM rating, multiply the bath's square footage by 1.07. Also, choose the quietest model you can find. The lower the sone (sound) level on the unit's rating plate, the better.
KITCHEN **Range hood fan** **Wall/ceiling fan**	Position a range hood fan from 21 to 30 inches above the burners. If possible, duct it to the outside. If not, combine a ductless range hood with a wall/ceiling exhaust fan.	To size range hood fans, multiply the number of linear feet your range occupies times 40 for against-the-wall installations (or 50 for peninsula or island configurations). The result equals the minimum CFM rating. To figure the CFM rating for wall/ceiling exhaust fans, multiply the square footage of the kitchen by 2. Choose a model with as low a sone rating as possible; anything over 8 is too loud.
COMBUSTION AIR **Air-to-air** **heat exchangers**	Mount these in the return-air side of the furnace, following the manufacturer's directions. Or, contact a heating and cooling service person to perform the job for you. Run ductwork from the outside to the air-intake portion of the appliance.	Typical CFM ratings for air-to-air, heat-exchanger fans range between 100 and 400, depending on house size.
Fresh-air ports	With existing fireplaces, bring the air to the base of the fireplace opening. With new installations, duct an air inlet port (available on most energy-efficient units) to the outside.	Use 4- to 6-inch rigid or flexible duct and a dampered vent.

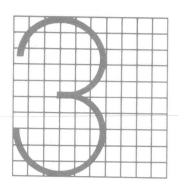

LEARN THESE SOLAR BASICS

Welcome home, sun! Just about any home can tap into this source of almost limitless, free nonpolluting energy. Once you have mastered a few basic principles about passive solar heating, you can open your house to sunlight, capture and store its warmth, and distribute heat when and where you need it. This chapter describes the best ways to accomplish these jobs.

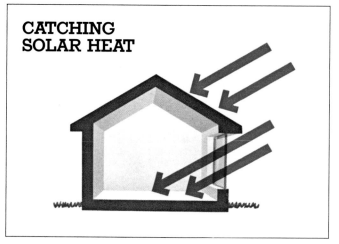

CATCHING SOLAR HEAT

The first step to harnessing the sun's heat is to bring the sun into your house. The most obvious, and most widely used, method is to install glazing in the south wall. This allows the winter sun to shine directly into south-facing rooms. Solar experts call this *direct gain* (see illustration *above*). Other popular methods are *indirect gain* and *isolated gain* (see pages 102-105).

You can install glazing in your roof—but only on the portions that face south and that are unobstructed, as was done on the roof shown *opposite*.

Keep in mind one important directional requirement. To be effective collectors, windows must face within 30 degrees east or west of true (not magnetic) south.

Choosing glazing
The following information will help you make a sensible decision about selecting glazing.
• *Fixed windows* are less expensive than the operable variety and lose less heat.

• *Wood-framed windows* lose the least heat through the frames. For metal frames, choose brands that have good thermal breaks between the outside and inside surfaces.
• *Double-insulated windows* (two panes of glass) are the best buys in most parts of the country.
• *Glass* is usually the most economical glazing. So-called low-iron glass allows in a bit more of the sun's heat than the ordinary kind, but its extra expense generally offsets this advantage. Other glazing materials—also more costly than ordinary glass—are polyester reinforced with fiber glass, clear acrylics, and clear polycarbonates.
• *The right amount of glazing* for each house will vary. However, a broad rule of thumb calls for south glazing equal to about 15-30 percent of the floor area you want to heat. Parts of the country with more sun should use the higher percentage and vice versa. (Remember, the more glass you have, the greater the potential for heat loss at night.)

STORING THE HEAT

Once you've enticed the sun into your home, the next step is to capture and store its heat. In winter's worst, you may want that warmth immediately. Usually, however, you need a way to store it till nighttime, when your sun furnace shuts down. For this you need *thermal mass*.

Thermal mass is any material that can soak up heat. Nearly every object in your house can do this; some materials, however, do it better than others. The table on this page compares the heat-absorbing abilities of several common materials. All of them work best if placed in the direct path of the sun, but even thermal mass that receives indirect sunlight can be effective.

Water works well

As the table indicates, water is one of the most effective choices. It's also the least expensive, though you do have to invest in containers of some kind. Metal drums and culverts, painted a dark color, are popular. Other options include furniture equipped with hidden water bags, and fiber glass thermal storage tubes.

Storage tubes range in size from 12 to 18 inches in diameter and 4 to 10 feet in height, are lightweight, and won't corrode. Just roll them into place and fill with water. To increase humidity during winter, simply leave the tops off.

The room *at right* has 12 such columns; each is 8 feet tall and 1 foot in diameter. Those shown here are translucent, but opaque containers work well, too.

COMPARING THERMAL MASSES

Substance	Relative Heat Capacity in BTUs*
Fir, pine, similar softwoods	330
Drywall	390
Quarry tile, brick, similar materials	710
Concrete	840
Water	1,870
Phase-change materials	9,500

*Heat storage capacity of one cubic foot of material heated from 70 degree F to 100 degrees F.

Masonry makes it, too

• *Concrete* and *concrete blocks* sponge up a lot of heat, and have a major advantage over water: They can serve as structural walls. Despite their solid reputation, poured concrete and blocks are highly versatile. Use them to make low divider partitions, hidden masses under built-in seating, floor bases, even complete wall systems.

• *Brick* is more attractive—and more expensive—than concrete. Use it as a veneer on interior walls. If you add brick (or other heavy materials), be sure the existing structure can support the extra weight.

• *Quarry tile, slate,* and similar masonry floorings add thermal mass (especially if laid over a concrete base) and make durable and decorative replacements for old floor coverings.

Phase-change materials

Phase-change materials (heat-absorbing mixtures of chemical salts) come in various containers—from flexible plastic pouches to 7-inch-high cans to narrow, 6-foot-tall columns. A phase-change material starts out in a solid form. It absorbs heat, then begins to melt when the temperature reaches about 80-90 degrees F. As the name indicates, it then changes from a solid into a liquid, storing a lot of heat in a small space. Later, the reverse occurs: The liquid releases its heat and reverts to a solid. Phase-change materials absorb heat better than most other kinds of thermal mass. However, they're also much more costly.

Storage capacity

The right amount of storage capacity depends on climate, the amount of south-facing glass and insulation in your house, and the type of system. For optimum storage capability, the rule of thumb is to use about 150 pounds of masonry mass or 60 pounds of water in direct sunlight for every square foot of south glazing. That's a lot of weight—more than you can probably find space for in an existing home. Lesser amounts of mass heat up more quickly and don't retain warmth for as long a period.

DISTRIBUTING THE HEAT

Now that you've collected and stored all that free heat, you have to find a way to distribute it as evenly as possible. You can do this in two ways: Take advantage of natural forces, or give Mother Nature a little help by adding a fan or two.

The natural way

How does heat travel without any help from fans, blowers, or other mechanical devices? Principally, in three different ways: convection, conduction, and radiation. The illustration *below* shows how each works in a passive solar system.

● *Convection* is simply the natural flow of heated air, which in a well-insulated house is up, but not out. In other words, warm air rises. If you provide a clear path for the air-flow, as indicated in the illustration, the heated air in a sunspace will rise and flow into the rooms behind the space. When the air cools, it will drop and return to the sun-space, only to become heated

again so it can begin another cycle. This convective loop will continue until the evening, when the space stops picking up heat.

Knowing how convection works can teach you some important lessons. For example, by cutting vents into walls and ceilings, you allow the heat to move as efficiently as possible. In the photo *at left,* sliding glass doors permit the heat to flow from the sunspace into the adjoining room. For that heat to travel into the northern-most room as well, you'd need to place vents in the back wall of the room pictured.

● *Conduction* is a kind of thermal domino effect. Study the storage wall in the illustration. As the sun strikes the outer face of the wall, the molecules on the surface heat up and pass along their warmth to the molecules behind them, a process that continues until the wall has conducted heat all the way to the inside face. The same action takes place in a floor serving as thermal mass.

● *Radiation* is probably the most familiar concept. When you hold your hand near a flame, you can feel the heat radiating toward you. The same thing happens in a thermal wall or floor that's been charged by the sun. When air in a space begins to cool, the mass begins to release its accumulated warmth. In the illustration *below,* the wavy lines from the floor and wall depict radiation.

Help is on the way

Many solar designers like to give the convective process a boost by inserting small fans inside some of the vents. Another way to enhance a passive system is to use a fan to force solar-heated air past indirect thermal mass. Heat transfers faster, making the mass more effective. For example, you can use precast concrete slab subfloors that have cores running from one end to the other. Fans pull solar-heated air through the concrete, and the heat is stored for later use.

An even more extensive hybrid is an underground rockbed that has heated air forced into it for storage. When you want to retrieve the heat, it will, depending on the installa-tion, radiate up through the floors or be convected to you via fans and ducts.

The large tube in the corner of the photograph *at left* is really an oversized duct. By convection, heat in the green-house rises to the peak of the tube where a fan pulls it down into a rock storage bin below grade. Another set of fans later distributes the warm air through the regular ductwork in the home.

HEAT-FLOW PATTERNS

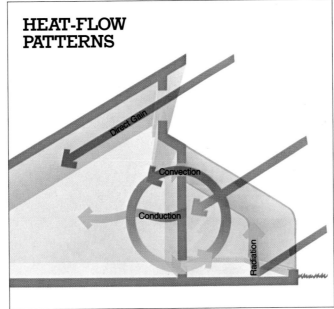

Direct Gain

Convection

Conduction

Radiation

CONTROLLING GAINS AND LOSSES

Like other systems, solar heating systems can spin out of control if you let them. Putting the sun's energy to work means, in effect, harnessing power so you can use it wisely. Doing *that* requires a careful plan.

Actually, you need two different plans—one to prevent excessive heat loss in winter, the other to guard against excessive heat gain in summer. The advice on this page tells how to retain as much wintertime warmth as possible; the information beginning on page 55 shows you how to handle summertime problems.

Leaky houses—those that in winter allow cold air in and warm air out—can undermine any heating system, solar or conventional. So the single most important step you can take is to tighten up your house. Weather-strip, caulk, and insulate every square foot of exterior surface, as explained in the preceding chapter.

After you've given your home a sound thermal barrier, focus your attention on the next major problem—glass. Yes, glass not only is your biggest ally during the day, it also is your biggest enemy at night and on cloudy days. South-facing windows—even if they're triple-glazed (R factor 2.6)—serve as two-way streets for heat gains and losses. Windows on the three other sides of your house are an even more serious problem. Fortunately, a solution is at hand: movable insulation.

Covering up

Movable insulation is nothing more than an insulating product you can use to cover or uncover a window with ease. At least five kinds are readily available: shades, draperies, shutters, interior storm windows, and pop-in panels. Some of them can be mounted outside the windows, but most are made for interior use. Two other types, thin films and small insulating beads, do their insulating inside the air space between two layers of glazing.

If you are considering a device you install on the outside —usually either plastic roller shades or an insulated unit that works like a garage door—you must keep rain and snow from slipping between the insulation and the windows it's shielding. But if you get a good, tight fit, the device can be even more effective than products mounted inside the house. One important disadvantage, of course, is that anything mounted outside may be less convenient to operate than a device operated from the inside.

Although not quite as effective, window insulation mounted inside your house is easier to reach and usually less expensive than the outside varieties. However, even though you don't have to worry about rain and snow, the seal between insulation and window must still be tight—this time, to prevent not only heat loss, but damaging condensation, as well. (The illustrations *at left* show two different ways to achieve a tight seal with sliding shutters.) Also think about fastening a reflective surface to the side of the insulation facing the glass (if the product doesn't already have this feature). It keeps heat from building up during summer. A similar problem doesn't exist, of course, for products mounted outside the house.

Putting it up

Do-it-yourselfers can install most window insulation. Generally speaking, shutters have the highest R values (in the 5 to 8 range), followed by shades (3 to 5), draperies (about 3), and interior storm windows and drapery liners (about 2 each). For three examples of energy-efficient shades, turn to pages 118 and 119.

Fit for both standard and extra-wide windows, the insulation shown *opposite* is a roll-up unit made of an interlocking series of PVC slats that slide up and down tracks at each side. You can hide it behind a valance or leave the unit exposed as it is here.

If you prefer to make your own window insulators, plans are available from several sources. Chapter 10 presents four different window-warming projects. Of these, one of the simplest is the pop-in panel, usually a sandwich of materials including fiber glass or rigid foam. You often just pressure-fit the panel inside the casing or stops (see page 140 to learn how to make one). When you want to uncover the windows, you have to store the panels or use them as decorative wall hangings, provided the outside layers are attractive enough.

SLIDING INSULATING SHUTTERS

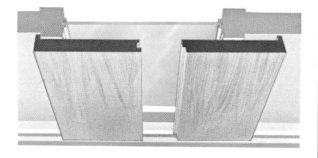

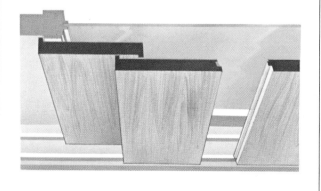

KEEPING COOL
IN SUMMER

SHADE TREE

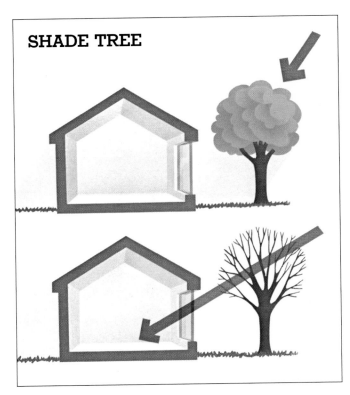

ROOF OVERHANG

Beginning to wonder whether all that south-facing glass will roast you in the summer? Don't worry; to keep cool during warm months just remember that the sun travels high in the sky during the summer and much lower during the winter. With that in mind, you can take steps to cut down on heat gain when it's hot outside (and, similarly, increase heat gain when it's cold).

First, you can install windows a special way: You can *recess* them to a depth that lets most of the summer sun strike the outside wall above the window, rather than penetrate the glass below. (This is another good reason to make sure your walls are well insulated.)

If recessed windows are not feasible, try other solutions. For example, tall deciduous trees on the south side of your house—east and west sides are also important—may already have solved the problem. As shown in the illustration *at top left,* their leaves will shade your house during the spring, summer, and fall, then drop to let the sun deliver its welcome warmth in winter.

Man the barriers!

Failing a natural solution, try adding man-made barriers. An old standby—the awning—is making a big comeback. Years ago, you could drive down many streets and see awnings on nearly every house. Awnings went out of style for a while, but today's homeowners are realizing the important role these coverings play: They can reduce heat gain through windows by up to 75 percent. If you do want to use awnings, buy those you

can open and close or easily remove when cold weather sets in. If you live in a climate that's sunny year round or want to shade a window that chronically gets too much sun, consider building a fixed awning like the one shown on pages 134 and 135.

Overhangs—or extensions of them—are also effective barriers. The best length for one depends on where you live and how far down glass extends from the top of the wall. (In northern latitudes, where the sun follows a lower path, an overhang should be slightly deeper than in southern regions.)

Before modifying the overhangs on your house, consider one disadvantage. Although an installation like the one illustrated in the drawing *below left* might block all of the sun on June 21 and, conversely, allow all of the sun past it on December 21, on many other days, the overhang will block or allow more sun than desired.

Adjustable overhangs can solve the problem. One of the simplest versions appears in the photo *opposite*. The unit consists of colorful canvas drawn across a framework by wires. In the winter, just remove the canvas and store it until spring or summer. Other successful designs incorporate slanted slats that you can pivot mechanically or remove manually and reinsert into grooves cut at different angles. Page 137 shows an adjustable overhead sunshade you can build yourself.

In a category all its own is the time-tested trellis—covered with vines in summer and devoid of them in winter. A lovely sight during the warm months, the trellis is nearly as effective as its adjustable counterparts.

(continued)

Outside controls are a big help in cooling your house. Even so, it still might become uncomfortably warm occasionally. Luckily, you *can* cool it down inexpensively, without resorting to an amp-eating air conditioner.

One way is to use an old-fashioned, but highly effective, paddle fan, such as the one shown *opposite*. Its long blades produce cooling, comforting breezes and prevent air from becoming stagnant. Most paddle fans are easy to install and cost little to operate. Many have five speeds, and some are reversible, so the same fan can pull warm air down from the ceiling during winter.

Time-lag cooling

Substantial amounts of thermal mass inside your home not only help absorb and release welcome heat in the winter, they also play an important role during the cooling season. Known as *time-lag cooling*, this method works well in climates where nighttime temperatures drop into the low sixties.

For best results, close up your house during the day, so the storage mass can absorb excess heat. At night, open your *highest* and *lowest* windows or vents, so natural convection can flush the house with cool air from the outside. The air will cool down the thermal mass, then exit upward as in the system illustrated *above*. You can give nature a hand by adding a fan or two at the high point of the convective cycle.

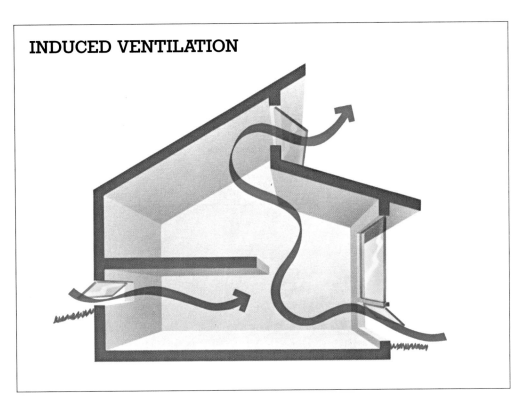

INDUCED VENTILATION

The sun can help cool, too

Remarkably, another cooling system is fueled by the sun. This system relies on the *chimney effect,* the natural tendency of hot air to rise. The goal is to create a hot spot high in your house where overheated household air can collect. Do this by removing at least part of a ceiling or by adding a chamberlike space, such as a cupola or some other kind of bump-up in the roof. Then install south-facing glazing (skylights or clerestories), and you have a pleasantly passive cooling system.

Here's how it works: Sunlight enters through the glazing and superheats the pocket of warm air. This causes the air to rise and exit through the glazing, if operable, or through a high vent or louver. If windows on the lowest level are open, cooler air enters the house and is pulled upward by the exiting air above. The result is a cooling breeze.

This concept also works for the *earth tube,* a still controversial solar cooling system. The objective in this case is to route cool air through an underground tube into your house. Natural convection pulls hot air into the tube through an aboveground intake. The tube, cooled by the surrounding earth, absorbs heat from the incoming hot air and causes moisture to condense and drain out through the bottom of the tube. The cool, conditioned air then sweeps into your house. Not all solar experts agree earth-tube cooling is effective.

Conventional means

You may want to install a more conventional *forced-ventilation* system for unbearably hot days. One standard approach is to reduce the amount of heat radiating downward from the attic. To do this, install soffit vents to serve as air intakes and add ridge vents or gable-end vents for exits.

Another alternative is a whole-house fan. Mount it in the ceiling of the uppermost level so the powerful blades pull hot, stale air into the attic, where it exhausts through vents. The airflow draws in fresh air through open windows in the lowest levels.

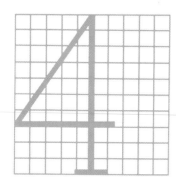

4

ADDING A SUNSPACE

One bright way to welcome the sun into your home is to build a solar addition, or sunspace. Constructed properly, a sunspace not only provides a ray of hope in the fight against rising energy bills, it also can serve as a cheery, light-filled living area. This chapter describes what you need to know if you're thinking of building a solar addition, how to make it useful year round, where plants fit in, constructing a sunspace with greenhouse components, and even how to add a sunspace to a condominium.

USE AS MUCH SUN AS YOU CAN

Put a solar addition on your house, and you'll have a chance to employ many of the sun-catching techniques described in Chapter 3. Like most other passive systems, a sunspace collects energy efficiently only if it's built to take the heat. That ability depends primarily on three considerations: location, size, and glazing.

Figuring out where to build a solar center is often a difficult question to answer (see Chapter 1); but if you can find the right spot, you've solved the biggest problem. Once you've determined where to build the sunspace, you need to decide how large it should be. Generally speaking, bigger is better, but deeper can be wasteful. You don't want to build a sunspace so deep that sunlight can't penetrate to the back wall. Exactly how deep it should be depends on the height of south-facing windows and how much roof glazing (if any) the space will have, as well as sun angles, shading, and other factors at your site.

The third consideration is the amount, type, and placement of glazing. Under the best circumstances, each square foot of south glazing will collect enough heat to warm 2 square feet of sunspace area. Thus, glazing is usually installed on the entire south wall but kept to a minimum on the east and west walls. An operable window to provide ventilation and a door that opens to the outdoors are good choices for those two sides.

The most popular kind of glazing is fixed glass, but if you want to hold down costs, you should also consider the other materials mentioned in Chapter 3. South glazing can be vertical, angled from the floor to the roof (as shown *below* and *opposite*), or angled from a knee wall to the roof. Glazing slightly angled— usually to a maximum of 60 degrees—collects more sun during winter, but vertical glazing is easier to install, maintain, and cover with insulation at night. Steeply sloped glazing usually has summer overheating problems. In cold climates, double-glaze sunspaces.

The sunspace shown here, attached to a Cape Cod that has to battle Maine's cold winters, boosts heating in the entire house—even on the coldest days of the year. Here there's no heat to store; the home uses it all immediately.

PLAN THE STRUCTURE CAREFULLY

Once you know how large your sunspace will be, how much glazing it will have, and where on your house it will go, you've figured out how to collect the sun. As you begin to plan the actual construction of the sunspace, your next decisions—determining how to store and how to distribute the heat—are equally important.

At this early stage, careful planning is essential. Be sure to answer these questions before you begin.

How will you hold heat?
Thermal storage should be part of any solar addition you plan to use day and night as a living space, or year round as a place to grow plants. By soaking up excess heat during the day and storing it for use at night, thermal mass helps even out temperature extremes, which might otherwise vary by as much as 80 degrees F in a sunspace.

The materials most suited to storing heat are: water in 55-gallon drums, bottles, or vertical tubes; masonry in the walls, floor, poured slab, or foundation of the sunspace; rock storage bins or beds isolated from the sunspace; and phase-change materials in rods or cans. (For more information about thermal mass, see pages 48 and 49.) In any event, consult a solar engineer to determine just how much and what type of thermal mass you need.

How will you keep heat in?
Like all energy-efficient construction, a sunspace must have adequate insulation. The colder the climate, the more insulation required. If you live where winters are very cold, frame the sunspace with 2x6s so you can stuff extra insulation into the walls and roof—R-27 walls and an R-40 roof are not uncommon. Be sure the vapor barrier is watertight, especially if you plan to grow plants in the sunspace. The extra humidity in a greenhouse can quickly ruin insulation if it sneaks through a hole in the vapor barrier.

If you anticipate using the foundation as thermal mass, use rigid foam to insulate around the *exterior* of the foundation. On the other hand, if you plan to use a rock storage bed below the floor of the sunspace, you could insulate around the foundation's *interior* instead.

What's right at night?
Movable window insulation dramatically reduces heat loss through the glazing at night, so unless your sunspace has no thermal storage and you plan to close it off from the rest of the house at night, window insulation is a must. (Pages 52 and 53, 118 and 119, and 140-145 show a variety of movable window treatments.)

How will you move heat?
If you plan to attach your sunspace to an existing exterior wall, it probably has windows, and possibly a door as well. Opening these will let solar heat flow into adjacent rooms.

However, if you can't establish an adequate convective cycle, you may also need vents and a fan to help pull the warmth through. If the common wall is uninsulated masonry, heat will also travel *through* it—this time, by conduction—and warm the living space. (For more information on distributing solar heat, see pages 50 and 51.)

A case in point
The sunspace added to the venerable Cape Cod home shown on these two pages collects 44 percent of the heat the house needs, thanks to a well-planned storage and distribution system. During the day, warmth is continually pulled from the sunspace into the house or into an isolated rock storage bin in the basement. The sunspace itself has no thermal mass, and because the room is closed off at night, window insulation is unnecessary. The glazing in the south wall, supported by a 2x6 frame on a 2x6 kneewall, is angled at 60 degrees.

ADDING A SUNSPACE

PLANNING FOR YEAR-ROUND USE

The kind of climate you live in determines, to some extent, the kind of roof you should plan for your sunspace. If your region has cold winters and hot summers, a solid roof is probably your best choice. Glazing in the walls can capture low-angled winter sunlight. South-facing walls gather the most heat when you want it, and in summer, when you don't, they receive less sun than east or west walls. Then, a solid roof deflects unwanted heat. But what if you need moderate amounts of solar heat throughout the year? In that case, overhead glazing might make sense.

Along the California coast, heat is often needed during all four seasons to take the chill off damp mornings. That's one big reason why the sunspace shown on these pages has a glazed roof; it admits warmth all year long.

Check the photograph *at right* and you can see that if the room overheats, sun can be screened from the space by lowering a king-size canvas shade. When heat does build up, a thermostatically controlled ceiling vent opens to dissipate it. Ventilation can be induced by opening the south and west casement windows. The design also includes an-

other way to bring in outside air. Opening a set of louvers (not shown) pulls up cool air from the shaded patio below.

Note, too, that this addition solves another problem you might be wondering about—how to add a sunspace to the main level of a home with a walkout basement. Raised on stilts, the new 16x24-foot greenhouse adjoins the kitchen, serving as a family room for all seasons.

Here the glazed roof is made up of prefabricated, double-glazed sections designed for commercial greenhouses. More about prefab greenhouses on pages 66 and 67, and 126 and 127.

ADDING A SUNSPACE

MAKING PLANTS PART OF THE SCHEME

Growing plants in a sunspace intended primarily for producing heat usually requires some trade-offs. But if you're willing to make a few concessions, you and your favorite plants can live together very happily.

As you can see, people and plants get along just fine in the sunspace add-on shown here. Besides providing a leafy environment, the sunspace serves as a transition between the basement and the main level pictured *at lower left.*

This sunspace is completely open to adjacent rooms, so the plants can share house heat. But this makes the room less efficient than one that could be closed off at night. Here are some of the other trade-offs you might need to consider for your sunspace:

● Vegetables and people require vastly different environments. If you'd like to produce a bumper crop of edibles, consider giving them sunspaces of their own, as explained in Chapter 9. Houseplants and flowering plants, however, can thrive in a sunspace you'll enjoy too. Also, you can start container plants from seed with excellent results.

● Even hardy houseplants can't tolerate temperature extremes, so you'll have to moderate temperature swings in your sunspace. Consider adding extra thermal mass to absorb excess daytime heat and release needed warmth in the evening. You may still have to provide nighttime heating, along with window insulation to minimize heat losses.

● You may need glazing in the roof as well as the walls if you want to grow plants year round. Plants require light no matter what the season.

● The air in a sunspace may be drier than most plants prefer, so you'll probably have to water them often.

● Plants need good ventilation year round, so you may want to add a fan to keep the air circulating around them.

CHOOSING A KIT-FORM GREENHOUSE

A greenhouse that comes as a kit can spare you the problems of designing and constructing a sunspace from scratch. Greenhouse kits include all the basic materials—glazing, framing members, fasteners, windows, and doors—and many provide completed roof and wall panels, interior and exterior finish materials, and ventilating fans, as well. In most cases, all you have to do is install the foundation; then just take out the step-by-step instructions, and put together your sunspace.

As with any major purchase, spend some time shopping around before you decide which greenhouse kit to buy. The decision may be especially difficult because you'll find a broad array of kits available, ranging from greenhouses built specifically for solar applications, to simple glass enclosures designed for horticultural use.

What makes a good one?

Basically, a sunspace kit should meet the same design criteria as a solar addition you would build from scratch. First, look at the roof and sidewalls. If they're all glass, you can be fairly sure the greenhouse won't function efficiently as a provider of solar heat. In most climates, the roof should be solid and well insulated to keep out summer sun. (To learn about the exceptions, see pages 62 and 63.)

Glass side walls also pick up too much heat in the summer. Moreover, they often *lose* more heat in winter than they gain. Instead of solid glazing on the sides, look for greenhouses with insulated walls and few openings. Check to make sure that doors, windows, and vents are well sealed.

Now, take a look at the south glazing. A greenhouse built to collect solar heat should have double glazing, with an airtight seal where the panes of glass join to the frame. Look for a frame (whether it's made of wood or metal) that has a thermal break—a strip of plastic or vinyl separating the inside and outside faces of the frame. Avoid designs that use clips on a bare metal framework to secure the glazing.

Some manufacturers offer heat storage and distribution systems, and insulated window coverings as options with the basic kit. If not, you can purchase them separately—thermal containers to store water, for example, or fans and controllers to distribute heat properly. A solar consultant can help you incorporate them when you install the greenhouse.

You can always adapt

Most greenhouse kits designed for horticultural use can't match the requirements described above. Horticultural greenhouses (especially older models) are often single-glazed and have curved-glass roofs. But if you're in love with the looks of a curved-glass greenhouse, you may be able to adapt one so you can use it as a sunspace. The solar addition shown *at left,* for example, only has prefab glazing components, not an entire greenhouse system. An insulated knee wall supports the glass on the south and west sides. To prevent unwanted heat from entering the space in summer, the owners place a trellis above the roof to shade the interior. They could also have used exterior roll-up blinds to accomplish the same thing. To see another horticultural greenhouse that has been converted into a sunspace, turn to pages 126 and 127.

BRINGING THE SUN INTO A CONDOMINIUM

Today, for millions of Americans home no longer is an isolated, single-family structure sitting on its own lot. Homeowners now live in many different kinds of housing—including duplexes, townhouses, and other dwellings that share common grounds and design aesthetics. If you own one of these and plan to add a sunspace, you'll most likely need to seek permission from your condominium association. Building what you want may mean cooperating—and often compromising— with your neighbors.

If your home is a condominium, read your association's legal documents establishing the rights and restrictions of home ownership in the community. You'll quickly discover what you can and can't do when you're thinking of remodeling or adding on.

If you want to make a change, you'll first probably have to petition the association's board of directors to gain approval for any building project. The board is most likely to be concerned about aesthetic aspects. Will the sunspace look out of place in the development? Or will it blend in visually?

If you can reassure the board of directors that the sunspace won't clash with the structures around it (perhaps by showing them architectural sketches) and if you can show that it won't infringe on the rights of other property owners, you may win the board's approval. Here, then, are some tips on how to make

your addition blend in with the neighborhood.

• Stick with traditional architectural shapes and styles that won't jar the aesthetics of the neighborhood. Use glass or clear acrylic glazing, not some unusual glazing such as polyester reinforced with fiber glass.

• Cover the sunspace with the same roof and wall materials used on your home.

• Add landscaping materials that match your neighbors' yards.

• If some homes in the development have bump-out windows or bays, use the same architectural style (on a larger scale) for the sunspace.

Both families in the duplex shown *above* converted part of their patios into sunspaces so unobtrusive that only the neighbors know the additions haven't always been there. In the interior of one, *at right*, the open wall between the kitchen and the sunspace marks the spot where sliding glass doors used to lead to the patio.

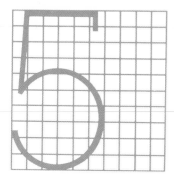

OTHER SOLAR STRATEGIES YOU CAN USE

At first glance, your home may may seem an unlikely candidate for solar retrofitting. After all, it probably wasn't sited for solar in the first place. Perhaps zoning restrictions or a lot line won't allow you to build a sunspace. Or maybe your main living areas face north, east, or west—not south. If you think your house is a solar misfit, don't give up hope. The pages that follow present yet other ways to give your house its place in the sun.

Some houses and lots are solar obstacle courses. If adding on would mean violating setback requirements, moving a garage, tearing out a swimming pool, or bulldozing irreplaceable shrubs and trees, then consider a simple remedy: Convert one or two existing rooms into sun-catchers by installing extra glass on the south side of the house.

For best results, add mass as well as glass. Even though an existing room may already be linked to a central heating system, try to incorporate thermal mass into the walls, floors, or other surfaces to store solar heat until it's needed. In addition, you may require sun shields and extra ventilation—operable windows, exhaust fans, or both—to stop heat buildup during summer.

A sun-warmed main room
Building an addition on the south side of this house, *above,* would have meant removing a venerable oak tree. So the homeowners "added" a sun-catcher simply by installing more glass in the existing south wall and carving out a 7x20-foot skylight in the roof.

The extra glazing brightens a spacious main room, *opposite,* one they created by combining the existing kitchen and dining room. To make way for the skylight, the ceilings in the old rooms were cut back 7 feet. A brick wall behind the wood stove serves as thermal mass, gradually releasing stored heat as the room cools down.

Automatic distribution
Excess heat collected in the room exits through a series of vents up top and is channeled to other rooms through large ducts in the attic. Each duct is equipped with a built-in fan. Special thermostats control the flow of heat—in the summer, above a certain temperature, it's automatically vented outdoors. Also in summer, the wide-spreading branches of the oak tree shade the skylight, and glass doors in the south wall slide open to admit cooling breezes.

CATCH THE SUN WITH A CLERESTORY

Adding large expanses of glass to a south wall is not always the best solution; it may mean sacrificing privacy or pumping the sun's warmth into little-used areas, such as laundry rooms or service halls. Nevertheless, you can use glass in other ways to capture the sun and put that energy exactly where it will do the most good. One alternative is to build a south-facing *clerestory* (pronounced "clear-story")—an outside wall, with windows, that rises above an adjoining roof.

If your roof is flat, a *cupola*-style clerestory may work well. (A cupola is a rounded vault, which, in this case, would rest snugly atop your roof.) If your roof slopes, a shed-roofed clerestory usually is a better choice.

Getting above it all
Solarizing the one-story contemporary ranch shown *at left and upper right* posed a problem because a garage adjoined the house along the south side, and the west side of the house faced the street. So the owners bumped up the roof over the entry hall (see illustration *at lower right*) and created a south-facing clerestory that pulls warm sunshine right into the center of the house all winter long.

The design of the entry's interior makes the most of all that free warmth. As winter sun flows in through the tall clerestory windows, it strikes the walls directly opposite. These walls, faced with adobe slump blocks, act as thermal mass that stores warmth during the day and releases it slowly into the house at night. A ceiling fan draws trapped heat downward from the clerestory and helps distribute it to other parts of the house. To reduce heat loss, the clerestory windows

are double-glazed, and the roof is insulated to R19.

Year-round energy savings
Adding a clerestory can cut cooling costs, too. Portions of the windows in this clerestory retrofit open and close, transforming the entry into a solar chimney that draws warm air out through the top of the

house and pulls cooler air in at ground level. A 4-foot overhang shades the windows from mid-March to late August, and the trellis and stained-glass window above the front door filter hot sun on the west side of the entry. In summer, the reversible ceiling fan adds to this chimney effect.

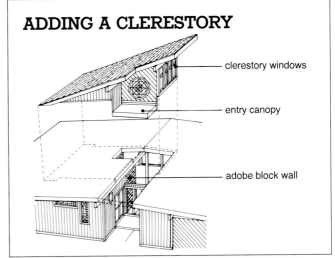

ADDING A CLERESTORY

clerestory windows

entry canopy

adobe block wall

USE SKYLIGHTS TO SCOOP IN WARMTH

Another way to direct the sun's heat into rooms that need it most is to add one or more skylights. Because they blend unobtrusively with the roof slope, you can add as many as you need without changing the basic lines of your house. In fact, skylights often require only the simplest of structural alterations—an opening between beams or rafters.

A split-level sun-catcher

The large skylight in the remodeled Victorian cottage shown *at upper right* forms the roof of a new 12x12-foot split-level entry that helps heat both upper and lower stories of the house. Constructed as an extension of the existing roof slope (see illustration *lower right)*, the skylight consists of six tempered glass panels mounted on a grid of 2x3 redwood framing. Beams made of Douglas fir support the grid; butyl tape and 2-inch-wide aluminum strips seal the joints between the panels. Note, however, that such a large skylight is advisable only where mornings are usually cool and damp. In most places, this much glazing would turn the interior into a solar oven during summer.

Circulatory system

To allow captured warmth to move freely, the owners replaced walls between the entry and adjoining rooms with the open railings and simple post-and-beam structure shown *at far right*. Quarry tile flooring in the entry and on the upper and lower levels of the house provides modest heat storage. Plus, canvas shades suspended on wires draw across the skylight to minimize heat loss at night or prevent heat build-up on warm summer days.

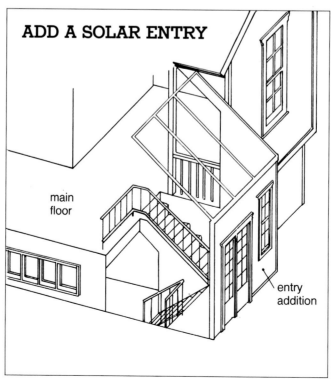

ADD A SOLAR ENTRY

main
floor

entry
addition

TURN A
MASONRY WALL
INTO A COLLECTOR

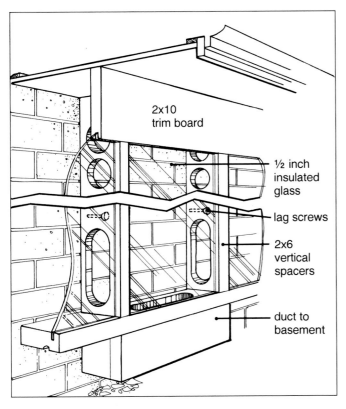

2x10
trim board

½ inch
insulated
glass

lag screws

2x6
vertical
spacers

duct to
basement

South-facing windows, clerestories, and skylights offer good ways to collect solar energy, but they still need thermal mass to hold the heat. Yet another way to solarize an existing house is to rebuild its southern exposure with an ingenious structure known as a *Trombe wall* (after its inventor, Dr. Felix Trombe), which stores as well as collects and helps circulate warmth to interior spaces.

Think of a Trombe wall as a flattened out sunspace. On the outside is a layer of glass; inside is a second, thick wall, usually made of masonry; between the two walls is a blanket of air—the filling in a solar sandwich. As the glass traps the energy of the sun, the air warms up and begins to serve the home's immediate heating needs. The masonry mass soaks up excess heat and holds onto it until the air cools again.

Since the mass in a Trombe wall consists of conventional building materials such as brick, stone, or poured concrete, any south-facing masonry wall that gets full sun in winter is a prime candidate for a Trombe wall retrofit. Also, Trombe walls are especially suitable for houses where no room exists to add a sunspace on the south side or where the need for privacy rules out large window walls.

A Trombe wall for a Victorian house
One big advantage of a Trombe wall is that it needn't be obtrusive, even on an older house such as the 70-year-old Victorian shown *opposite*. Here, there's no room between the house and driveway for a full-size sunspace, and large window walls would have exposed this side to neighbors.

The walls of the structure are solid brick, so they were easily converted to a Trombe wall. The owners painted the brick dark brown, then added a layer of ½-inch-thick insulated glass panels. The panels are mounted on a series of 2x6s attached to the brick wall with lag screws and masonry anchors (see the drawing *at upper left*).

Sun-warmed air passes from panel to panel via 2½-inch-diameter holes cut in the spacers, and is drawn into the house through a system of ducts and a low-voltage fan. Another fan pulls cool air from rooms on the north side of the house and feeds it back into the Trombe wall through ducts in the basement ceiling. Each fan operates on thermostatic controls—and costs only about two dollars a month to run.

Bays bring in more heat
During the day, additional warmth flows directly into the house through bay window units installed over the existing openings. Behind one of these bays, a pair of old kitchen windows gave way to the large greenhouse-style opening shown *at lower left*.

Besides supplying direct-gain solar warmth, the bay window units help blend this retrofit with the home's original styling. Their projecting shapes lend sculptural depth to the Trombe wall glazing, and their vertical proportions echo those of other door and window openings.

ADD A SOLARIUM THAT CAPTURES THE SUN

Where space permits, the best strategy may be a solar retrofit that expands your living area. With this kind of approach, you get two benefits for the price of one: lower utility bills and extra breathing room.

The tower-shaped solarium added to this two-story frame house in Minnesota, shown *at upper right,* is an excellent example. Although measuring only 9x12 feet, it traps as much energy as an addition twice its size. Rising the full height of the house, the solarium meets the sun head-on in three directions—south, southeast, and southwest.

Make room

The lower level of the solarium, shown *at lower right,* adds space in the kitchen for casual dining. The upper level, shown *opposite,* functions as an airy plant bay in the second-floor study. Sun-warmed air from the dining area rises through the metal-grate floor in the plant bay and circulates to other parts of the house via large cutouts in the wall of the study. In the day, this heat flow is generated by direct gain, but at night it radiates from the eating area's quarry tile floor, which acts as thermal mass.

Movable insulation

To conserve stored heat, foil-backed insulating shades mounted in the plant bay automatically unroll to the tile floor below. Foil-backed shades also insulate other large areas of glass on the south side of the house. (For more about insulating windows, turn to pages 118 and 119 and pages 140-147.)

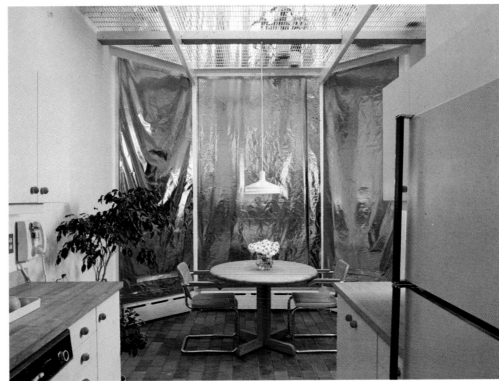

BUILD AN ADDITION THAT HEATS ITSELF

Some solar retrofits are completely separate rooms that heat themselves and pump bonus warmth into other parts of the house. If your house has space for an addition to its south side, your best bet may be a new, self-heating room.

Sun porch

A solar addition may be just about anything—kitchen, dining room, family room, even a workshop—but perhaps the simplest type is a glassed-in porch. The 18x18-foot solarium on the south side of this two-story New England home, *at right,* provides comfortable living space year round. It also helps heat the rest of the house during winter.

An important feature of this addition is the unique stair-stepped ceiling visible in the interior photograph *below.* The effect comes from thin sheet-aluminum "treads" and clear glass "risers" pitched to admit sunlight in winter and bounce it back into the sky in summer. The roof's exterior surface consists of corrugated plastic panels that provide a weather-tight cover without blocking the sun's rays. The roof rises to cover the second-story windows, allowing heat from the porch to flow into both levels of the house when windows in the existing exterior wall are opened.

Built-in heat storage

Part of the solar warmth collected by the roof and the floor-to-ceiling glass walls is stored in the porch floor and the brick veneer on the existing wall. The floor consists of hexagonal quarry tile flooring set on a poured concrete pad. Because the homeowners wanted the porch to be on the same level as the main living areas in their house, the floor pad itself was constructed above grade on cylindrical concrete piers. The piers provide ample support for the extra weight of the porch floor and—unlike wooden posts or timbers—will never rot out and need replacing. Insulation under the floor pad helps prevent stored heat from escaping to the outside. Even if you decide to pour a pad on grade level, insulate well around its perimeter to minimize heat loss.

On cloudy days and cold winter nights, a woodburning stove supplies backup heat; on hot summer days excess warmth moves out through the sliding glass doors on either side of the new solarium.

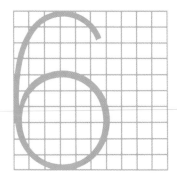

SELECTING SOLAR COLLECTORS

Those strange new add-ons you're noticing on more and more rooftops, walls, and lawns probably are solar collectors of some kind or another. Whatever their sizes or shapes, they're hard at work converting the sun's free rays into some kind of household energy. In each case, these sun grabbers are helping families reduce their bills from—and dependence on—the local utility company. Most collectors you see now are heating household water; but a growing number are heating living spaces as well. A few are even hard at work converting sunlight to electricity.

Don't let the name "thermosiphoning air panel" intimidate you. This simple device is actually one of the most basic solar collectors on the market. It's a space heater, and it's effective. A row of these mini-furnaces mounted on the south wall of your house can keep your rooms comfortably warm as long as the sun is shining.

You can buy the basic unit ready-made for between $500 and $700, plus installation. Sizes vary, but you'll generally be working with a shallow metal box about 7 feet tall, 3 feet wide, and 4 inches thick. The major components are glazing, an absorber plate, insulation, a couple of vents, and an optional fan.

The concept is simple. Just cut vent openings—one high, one low—into the south wall of your house and mount the module so it covers the vents. Then let the sun do its work. The drawing *below* shows what happens. As the sun shines through the glazing and strikes the absorber, heat builds up. Warmed air inside the collector rises and flows through the top vent into the living space. This airflow, in turn, pulls cooler household air into the lower vent to continue the convective cycle. A thin plastic flap on the bottom vent prevents reverse airflow.

The 1,900-square-foot house *opposite* has a total of six solar panels (two out of camera range at right) mounted on its south-facing wall. When the temperature inside the panels reaches 110 degrees, fans automatically begin pushing warmed air into the house.

To learn how to make your own solar collector, turn to pages 148 and 149.

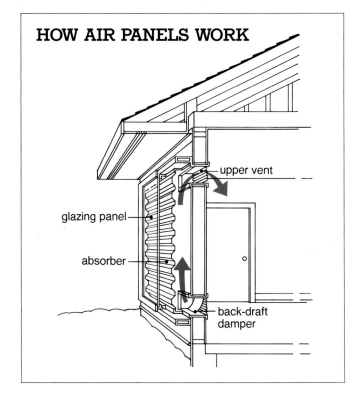

HOW AIR PANELS WORK

upper vent

glazing panel

absorber

back-draft damper

SELECTING
SOLAR
COLLECTORS

PASSIVE
HOT WATER
SYSTEMS

The simplest systems that heat household water are "passive heaters." Like the space heaters on the previous pages, passive water heaters also depend on the age-old principle that warm water rises. These systems don't have any pumps or moving parts. Instead, the tendency for heated water to seek its highest level creates the convective flow that makes passive systems work.

One popular unit in the Sun Belt is the model shown *at left.* Its collectors and tank can replace a standard water heater in climates that have mild winters.

Cold water enters the collectors' bottom, rises as it is heated, then enters the insulated tank up top, ready for use.

The average price, including installation, is about $4,000. At that cost, and assuming utility rates remain at today's level, the system would pay for itself in two to five years.

Another basic unit is the passive pre-heater shown *at upper right.* Unlike the other example, this one supplements rather than replaces your water heater. It has no collectors attached to it; instead, the entire package—double glazing over two 30-gallon tanks, backed by insulation—is one giant collector of sorts.

The drawing *at lower right* shows how cold water enters the bottom of the first tank, is heated, exits through the top of the second, and feeds into your existing water heater.

For northern states, optional thermostatically controlled electric pads around the tanks keep the water from freezing at night. The complete unit costs about $1,500. For that outlay, a typical household could get about 50 percent of its hot water from the sun.

TWO-TANK PASSIVE SYSTEM

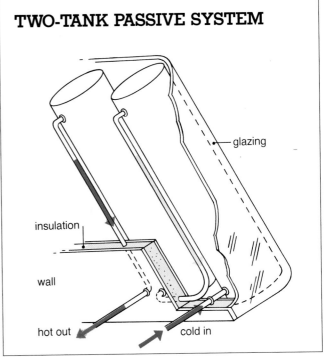

glazing

insulation

wall

hot out   cold in

ACTIVE HOT WATER SYSTEMS: OPEN LOOP

DRAINDOWN SYSTEM

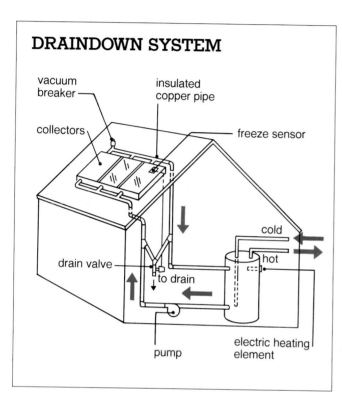

vacuum breaker

insulated copper pipe

collectors

freeze sensor

cold

hot

drain valve

to drain

pump

electric heating element

DRAINBACK SYSTEM

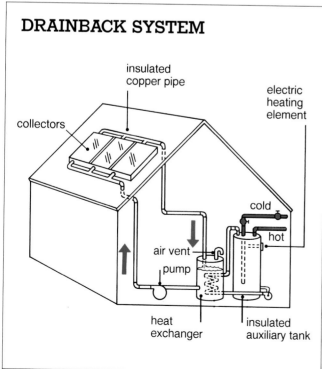

insulated copper pipe

electric heating element

collectors

cold

hot

air vent

pump

heat exchanger

insulated auxiliary tank

Active solar systems bring into play devices such as pumps and controllers. Additionally, to prevent the freeze-up problem that exists in all but the mildest climates, manufacturers of "open-loop" systems add equipment that automatically drains the water from the system in freezing weather.

The term *open loop* refers to water heating systems that are vented to open air (otherwise they wouldn't drain efficiently). Manufacturers of these systems use two basic draining methods: *draindown* and *drainback*. In a draindown system (see illustration *at upper left*), water that flows through the collectors to be heated is the same water that flows to your kitchen, bathrooms, and laundry. But in a drainback system (see illustration *at lower left*), a separate loop flows from the collectors to a storage tank where a heat exchanger captures the heat for your household water.

In draindown configurations, the system, normally filled by water pressure from your water heater, is drained by a drain valve. When the collector temperature drops to a specified low point, the valve opens and dumps the water from the collector into a drain. The photo *at right* and the upper drawing illustrate a typical draindown system. A six-panel unit as shown can supply about 60 percent of the hot water for a family of four at an initial cost of about $5,000.

In a drainback system, freeze protection is slightly different: When the collector temperature drops to a certain point, the pump that normally forces the water up into the collectors stops, allowing the collectors to drain back into the storage tank.

ACTIVE
SOLAR SYSTEMS:
CLOSED LOOP

Closed-loop systems are the most popular choice in areas where freezing temperatures are common-place. That's mainly because the fluid that circulates through the system is often a 50/50 mixture of water and glycol antifreeze, which won't freeze even if temperatures reach -30 degrees F.

A closed-loop configuration can heat living spaces, pools, hot tubs, radiant-type floors, or tap water.

When used to heat a family's household water, as is the case in the two examples shown here, the system functions as shown in the drawing. Because the antifreeze liquid is undrinkable, it circulates in a separate loop that isolates it from the household water. The liquid is heated by the sun, then pumped through a heat exchanger. The exchanger often is inside an insulated storage tank, as shown, though it can have a separate mounting. (If so, a second pump circulates the storage-tank water through the isolated exchanger to extract heat from the transfer fluid.) Though the illustration shows a one-tank system, a few systems use two. In those cases the tank containing the exchanger has no backup heating element; rather it serves as a pre-heater for the existing water heater.

The unit pictured *at left* cost its owners about $3,600 and produces more than half of the hot water they need; an electric element in the solar tank supplies the remainder.

The system shown *at upper right* cuts its owners' hot water bills by 65 percent, in return for an investment of $8,700 (dormer included). Backup heat comes from a gas burner in the top third of a 120-gallon water tank; the solar system heats the lower 80 gallons.

THE ANTIFREEZE LOOP IS CLOSED

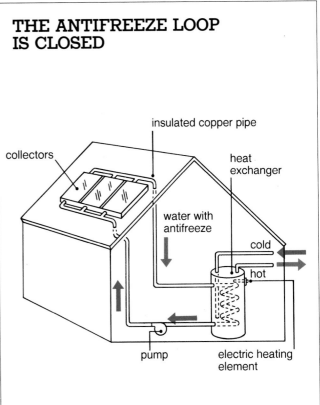

insulated copper pipe

collectors

heat exchanger

water with antifreeze

cold

hot

pump

electric heating element

ACTIVE SOLAR SYSTEMS: AIR

Not all solar collectors circulate liquids. Some manufacturers produce air systems, though few are sold solely for heating household water. That's because an air system needs an air-to-liquid heat exchanger to warm the domestic hot water, and such exchangers are less efficient than other types.

When an air system helps heat living spaces or both living areas and household water, however, it can be an effective choice. In those solar units that supply only heat to living spaces, a fan simply moves air through passages in the collectors; there the air picks up heat, then journeys through the house via ducts.

Some systems can store heat when it isn't needed right away. These setups usually channel the warmed air from the collectors to an insulated bin of uniformly sized rocks. To retrieve the heat for nighttime use, fans drive household return air through the rock bin and out warm-air ducts into the living spaces.

Storing systems require rather complicated controls with motorized dampers; the cost of this equipment—and of the rock bin—make this option substantially more expensive than the non-storing units on the market. As a result, the systems without any storage provide the most BTUs for the investment—but with the tradeoff that heat is available only when the sun shines. On the other hand, systems that can store excess heat can supply warmth long after the sun sets.

Systems that heat both space and tap water make good use of the sun year round. The unit in the photo *at right* is a good example. (Though the collectors pictured

are curved, air systems are also available with flat panels.) Simply by setting the thermostat at the normal household temperature, the homeowner can direct this system to concentrate on space heat. When the house is comfortably warm, a controller detours the solar heat to a pre-heat tank for the domestic hot water. By lowering the thermostat to a setting below the normal level, the owner can instruct the system to deliver all of its solar BTUs to heat domestic water.

The illustration shows the equipment's layout. When in the space-heating mode, the system pulls room air up through ducts to the collectors; there it absorbs heat, then travels through a separate set of ducts back to the living space. When the domestic hot water cycle comes on, selected dampers open and close, rerouting the air in a closed loop between the collectors

and the air-to-water heat exchanger.

Water circulating via pipes that snake through the heat exchanger picks up solar heat from the air and returns to the insulated pre-heat tank. As 140-degree water is drawn from the conventional water heater, 100-degree solar-heated water from the pre-heat tank replaces it and is warmed by gas or electricity to 140 degrees. Meanwhile, 50-degree supply water enters the pre-heat tank, ready to be warmed by the sun to 100 degrees.

With a four-panel system like this one, a homeowner in a northern state can expect the sun to contribute about 30 to 40 percent of the space and water heating needed during winter, nearly all of the water heating needed during the summer, and a good share of both during the spring and fall. Cost is about $10,000.

HOW AN ACTIVE AIR SYSTEM WORKS

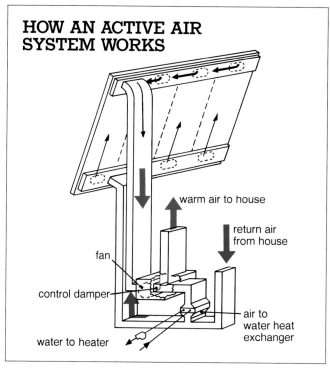

warm air to house

return air from house

fan

control damper

water to heater

air to water heat exchanger

PHOTOVOLTAIC
SYSTEMS

One of the most exciting solar collectors available contains no pipes or ducts. This collector consists of row upon row of *photovoltaic* (PV) solar cells designed to create *electricity.*

In photovoltaics language, a group of cells is called a *module.* Several modules ganged together form a *panel,* and all the panels together create an *array.* But the system's heart is the thin little cell that converts sunlight into electricity.

You can expect a solar cell to produce most of its power from about 9 a.m. until 3 p.m., and hit its peak at noon on a sunny day. But though the sun constantly delivers about 100 watts of energy to every square foot on earth, today's solar cells can convert only about one-eighth of it into electricity. As improvements continue, cell efficiency should improve, and cost per kilowatt will drop, perhaps dramatically.

The only cost-effective systems in service today are the stand-alone versions (installations in remote areas where the cost to bring in power is prohibitive). In spite of this, however, over 90 percent of all PV systems operating in the United States are utility-interactive—that is, they are wired into the local utility.

Check the upper drawing for a typical stand-alone system. Direct-current power from the array travels through a battery either to DC loads or through an invertor to AC loads. Conversely, the utility-interactive system illustrated in the photo *at left* and in the lower drawing has no batteries but does have more control devices than do stand-alone versions. The system illustrated creates enough power for the average home and sells any excess to the utility. The system's cost: $31,000.

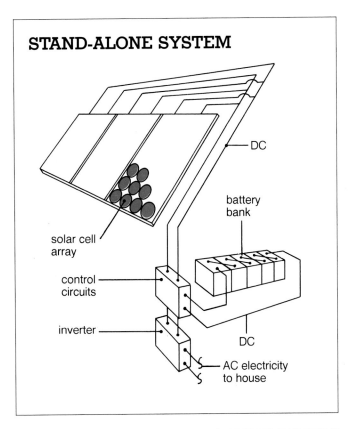

STAND-ALONE SYSTEM

DC

battery bank

solar cell array

control circuits

inverter

DC

AC electricity to house

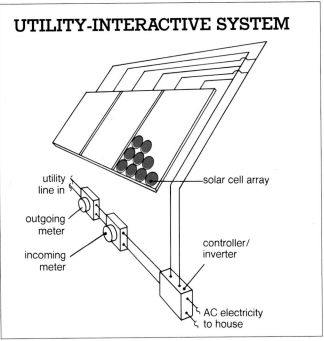

UTILITY-INTERACTIVE SYSTEM

utility line in

outgoing meter

incoming meter

solar cell array

controller/ inverter

AC electricity to house

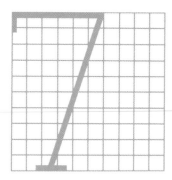

PLANNING A NEW SOLAR HOME

The preceding chapters explain basic solar principles and discuss how you can apply them to an existing house. This chapter takes you into a whole new world: building a solar home from the ground up. It tells you how to select a site, how to pick a plan, and how to choose from the ever-expanding array of solar designs, with emphasis on the advantages and disadvantages of each system.

Natural forces can work both for and against a solar home, so look for land that enjoys a lot of sun.

Before you begin looking for a site, first consider the basic weather patterns in your area of the country. The United States has four major climate zones—temperate, cool, hot/arid, and hot/humid (see the map, *opposite, below*).

The chart also *opposite, below,* should give you a general idea of the kind of site to look for, depending on the climate in your area. At the least, it will help you quickly eliminate some locations and pay closer attention to others that might work.

Also included in the chart are design strategies that apply to each region. Use this information when you're about to select a particular type of solar heating system. (Descriptions of each system begin on page 100.)

You can obtain more specific information about regional climates from the National Oceanic and Atmospheric Administration, located at the National Climactic Center in Asheville, North Carolina. For a small fee, this government agency will send you a detailed summary of the climate in your area.

Weather-wise
More specifically, it'll pay to become familiar with two basic meteorological concepts.

• *Degree-days.* This is a numerical measure of how cold any one area is, based on its mean temperature below a given point, usually 65° F. (Three examples: Des Moines, Iowa, has 6,700 degree-days; Atlanta, Georgia, 2,800; Caribou, Maine, 10,200). Thus, the higher the number of degree-days at your location, the more emphasis you should place on insulating and tightening up your home, and the greater the likelihood that solar heating can save big money on energy bills.
• *Percent possible sunshine.* If this figure is less than 50 percent, solar systems probably aren't a good economic choice for you. The map *opposite, above,* shows the number of degree-days and the percent of possible sunshine in each of the country's four different major climate regions. Bear in mind, however, that these figures may not apply precisely to a potential building site. Natural and artificial features can alter climate dramatically, creating "microclimates" that differ from one site to another, and even from one part of a site to another.

The information on the next two pages will help you define a microclimate that's suitable for solar living.   *(continued)*

REGIONAL DIFFERENCES: PERCENT POSSIBLE SUN AND DEGREE-DAYS

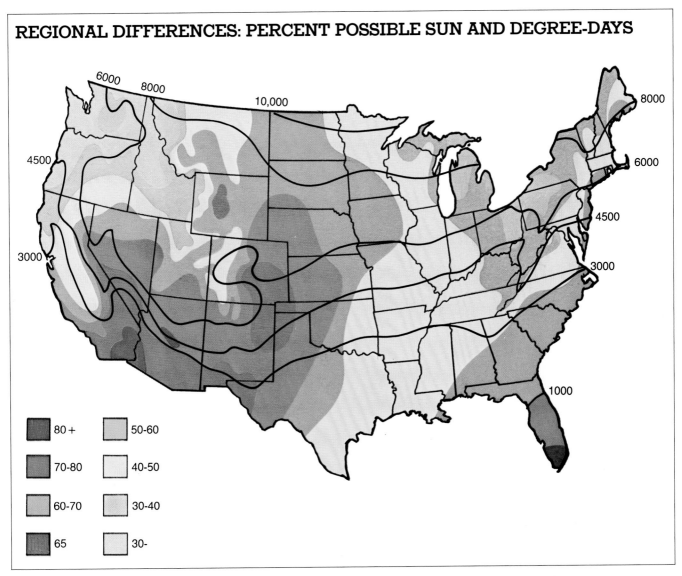

Legend:
- 80 +
- 70-80
- 60-70
- 65
- 50-60
- 40-50
- 30-40
- 30-

U.S. CLIMATE ZONES

CLIMATE ZONE	BEST SITING	POOR SITING	DESIGN STRATEGIES
Temperate	Gentle southern slopes with scattered deciduous trees.	Windy ridges, steep north or west slopes, unventilated depressions.	Maximize winter sun; provide shade in summer.
Cool	Sheltered south-facing slopes; evergreen trees to north.	Exposed ridges, hillcrests, north or west slopes, hollows, windy sites.	In winter maximize solar warmth and reduce the effect of winds.
Hot/Arid	Flat land, shallow north slopes, southeast slopes.	Southwest or northwest slopes, steep north slopes, hot valley bottoms.	Emphasize midday shade. Southern orientation important for high altitudes.
Hot/Humid	Mature woodland on any gentle slope, flat sites, breezy sites.	Sites without breezes, steep slopes, treeless sites.	Maximize shade and encourage air movement throughout the day.

The United States is made up of the four basic climate zones shown above. Within each zone exist many localized climatic variations.

95

SELECTING A SITE
(continued)

SITE ANALYSIS CHECKLIST

ENERGY-RELATED FEATURES

Yes No

- ☐ ☐ Will your home enjoy good access to the winter sun?
- ☐ ☐ Will the house get enough sun when trees begin to grow or new buildings go up on adjacent properties?
- ☐ ☐ Will it have shelter from winter winds?
- ☐ ☐ Can summer breezes reach the site?
- ☐ ☐ Is the site elevated out of depressions where cool air tends to pool?
- ☐ ☐ Are there deciduous trees to the south to provide summer shading?
- ☐ ☐ Are large bodies of water nearby to help lessen temperature variations?
- ☐ ☐ Is the least expensive fuel (for the area) available on the site?

GENERAL SITE FEATURES

- ☐ ☐ Can you accept any legal stipulations that apply to the site (restrictive covenants, zoning regulations, easements)?
- ☐ ☐ Is good water already available, and, if not, can you obtain it easily? (Check with neighbors.)
- ☐ ☐ Can you connect to sewer lines; if not, is the soil suitable for a septic system? Is the soil strong enough to support the weight of a house?
- ☐ ☐ For electricity, is a utility pole or underground cable nearby?
- ☐ ☐ Is there a good access road, and, in cold climates, can you handle the drifted snow?

DEVELOP A TOPOGRAPHICAL MAP

If a site scores well, the next step is to develop a map of the lot, something best left to a professional's skill and training. An architect will do it as part of the overall design, but any qualified surveyor or certified engineer also should be up to the task. All maps should include the following features.

Potential sun blockers
- trees to the south, indicating height and whether they're evergreen or deciduous
- the location and height of tall objects to the south that could cast winter shadows on the house

Winds
- show direction of predominant winter and summer winds
- major hills and ravines that can channel winds

Topography
- elevations and contours
- slopes, flat areas, depressions
- existing trees and buildings
- streams and bodies of water

Soil types
- type of soil at several locations (sandy, clay, loam, rocky, or combinations

Existing utilities
- location of electric, water, gas, sewer

Access
- location of main road and proposed access route

Legal restrictions
- setbacks—the required distances between house and lot lines
- all restrictive-covenant and easement agreements with neighbors

Use the completed map as a guide—your most valuable one—to buying a lot and siting your solar home on it.

How do you select the site that's right for your solar house? Check the following vital signs.

- *Natural vegetation.* Trees can determine whether a site is suitable for a solar home. Deciduous trees are a big help if they're to the south of a house. They provide shade during summer and allow sunlight through in winter. Dense stands of timber, however, may have to be thinned out if their leafless branches cast too many shadows in winter. Evergreens are valuable, also. To the north, they block cold winds. To the east or west, they stop the sun from scorching a house in summer.

- *Topography.* Halfway up a south-facing slope is an ideal spot for solar designs. North-facing slopes and sites at the bottom of hills tend to be shaded and cold in winter. Sites at the top of hills, regardless which slope they're on, usually are cold because they are exposed to wind. The site plan shown *opposite* illustrates how terrain affects the natural forces working on a house.

- *Wind.* Wind can rob a house of heat in the winter. Generally, the coldest winds blow from the north, so look for a site featuring natural windbreaks—hills or dense vegetation—that provide solid protection at this time of the year. In summer, a good site allows cool breezes to flow easily. Study the site for features that might block any cooling breezes.

Using the checklist
Answer the questions in the checklist *at left*, then count up the number of checks in the "yes" boxes. The higher this number, the better suited a site is for collecting solar energy.

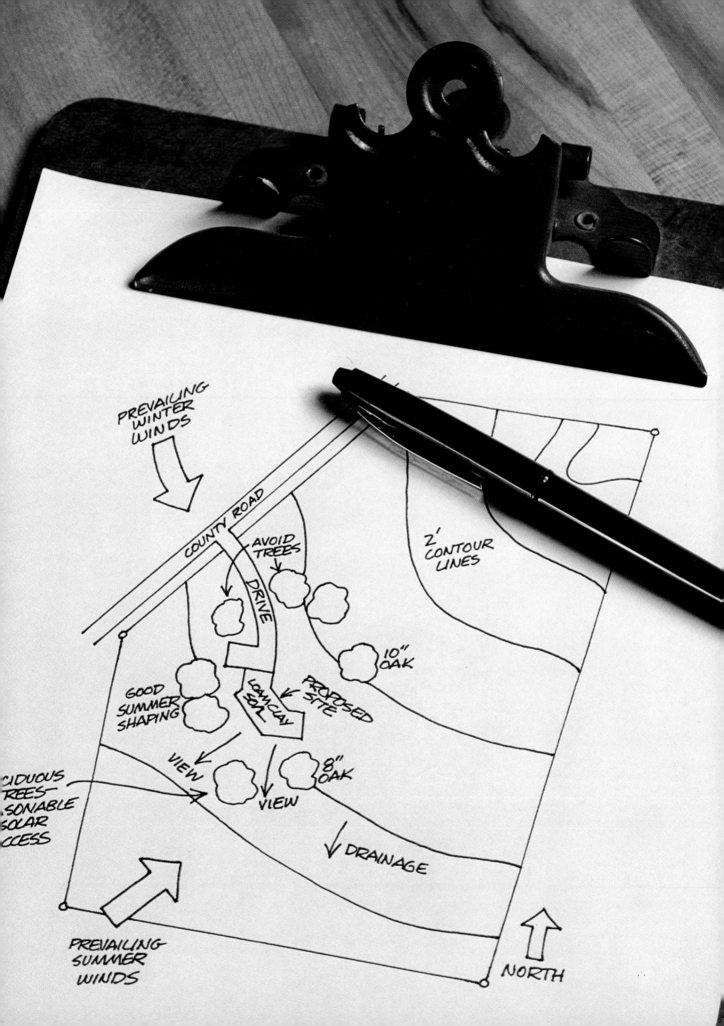

PICKING A PLAN

Not everyone can afford to work with an architect. For a house exactly tailored to your needs and tastes, only a professional will do. But just as you can have off-the-rack clothes modified to fit, using a set of mail order or builder plans can give you satisfying results. The key to success with ready-made plans—for any kind of house, solar or conventional—lies in selecting a plan suited to your site. Then, if necessary, you can make changes, adapting it to your specific needs.

Plans of action

When you study a set of plans, make sure the design is compatible with your site's characteristics. Look for major window areas that face the best views. (If you've selected a good solar site, this usually means south.) Windows that open should face the predominant summer breezes, with another set of windows on the opposite side to help set up cross ventilation.

The basic shape of the house should fit your site. If it's on a steep slope, look for a design with a walk-out basement, or in hot and humid climates, one that sits on a pole foundation.

A heavily wooded site requires a house with a compact foundation if you want to minimize the number of trees that must be felled. On a site with bedrock or boulders near the surface, the same strategy helps keep building costs down.

Finally, make certain the entries to the garage and house are easily accessible. How you position the house will go a long way toward determining that.

MODIFYING STANDARD PLANS

MINOR CHANGES

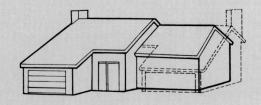

- "Flopping" floor plans for left-to-right mirror images
- Relocating a garage entry
- Adding a basement or changing the proportion of basement to slab area (provided there is room for stairs)
- Adding double- or triple-glazed windows
- Adding a wood stove or fireplace
- Changing an exterior finish
- Adding decks or porches

MODERATE CHANGES

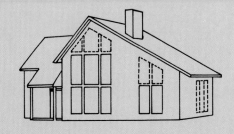

- Moving a few windows
- Changing sizes, types of windows
- Increasing levels of insulation beyond 3½ inches in walls
- Extending overhangs
- Adding more southern glass and heat-absorbing material to increase passive solar capability
- Simple changes to floor plans
- Adding a new wing
- Converting a basement to prime living space

MAJOR CHANGES

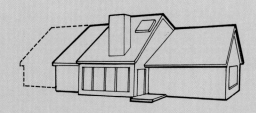

- Extensively relocating rooms or increasing floor area
- Adding another story
- Changing the basic shape and form of the house
- Changing the location of the house's entry (other than flopping the entire plan)
- Relocating a large number of the windows

Will the plan suit your life-style?

Matching a plan to your site is crucial, but so are your family's needs. Here are some other points to keep in mind before you decide on a set of plans.

• *Allocation of space.* The size of a house is less important than the way you live in the space inside. Using your present residence and furnishings as a guide, think about how much space you want to allocate for each room. If your budget is limited, make conservative estimates. At the same time, don't lock yourself into the present. If you plan to have three children, for instance, make at least one bedroom large enough for two twin beds.

• *Need for personal space.* Do you require peace and quiet for study or work? Then look for a plan with a larger-than-average master bedroom, or one with a study tucked away from noisy areas.

• *Resale potential.* Unless you are building a retirement retreat, you'll probably want to sell your house in the future. Don't build one dramatically larger or smaller than others in your area. In general, three-bedroom houses sell faster than those with two bedrooms.

• *Maintenance costs.* Using materials you don't have to replace or refinish every few years is a good investment. Though you'll spend more initially, the savings over the years are usually worth it.

• *Personal preferences.* Try to match the plan to the activities you enjoy, rather than alter your behavior to accommodate the design. If you or someone in your family likes to cook, look for a plan with a big kitchen; and if the chef likes privacy, look for separate dining and cooking areas.

Energy considerations

If the plan you like isn't specifically designed for solar heating, it can still be energy efficient. The best plans allow you to put living and sleeping areas to the south, working areas to the north, east, or west. Large windows should face south; smaller ones, north. If your summers are hot, west walls should have the fewest windows because that's where the sun shines longest and hardest.

If you live in a cold climate, one other thing to consider is a feature becoming standard in many parts of the country: exterior walls framed with 2x6s instead of the usual 2x4s. The extra space allows for more insulation.

A change of plans

No ready-made plan is going to provide *exactly* what you want. All need at least some modifications. Most builders, architects, and engineers are qualified to alter a set of plans to your specifications. However, to keep down the cost of redrawing the plan, try to make only minor or moderate changes. The chart *opposite* explains the various degrees of alterations.

HOW TO WORK WITH AN ARCHITECT

The best way to get a house that makes the most of your site is to hire an architect. If you're hesitating to contact one because you aren't sure what to expect, here's what architects do and how they set their fees.

Select an architect just as you would any other professional whose services you need. Be sure to get recommendations—from friends, builders, associations, or banks—and make a round of visits. Ask to see houses the architect has designed, and discuss generally the project you have in mind. Be sure to include your proposed budget in the discussions. Then choose an architect whose work and way of working appeal to you.

Pay as you go

An architect's fee is usually a percentage of the building budget, not including land cost. A standard rate is 8 to 15 percent, with the higher percentage applying to smaller projects. Often you also must add out-of-pocket costs such as blueprinting fees, telephone calls, and expenses for making trips to your site.

You pay the fee as various stages of the design work are completed, starting with an initial retainer that's usually 5 percent of the total amount.

Normally, an additional 15 percent of the fee is due after the architect completes the schematic de-sign. This phase is the most important; the schematic represents the basic concept for your house. After a process of review and modification, the architect fleshes out these sketches.

You pay 20 percent more of the fee when the preliminary design is finished. By now, most of the myriad details—the layout of the kitchen, heating and cooling system, placement of electrical outlets, and so on—are being worked out. Also included at this stage are perspective drawings that show the client what the interior and exterior will actually look like.

When the final design is finished, another 40 percent of the fee is due. At this stage, the architect draws the blueprints used to build the house. Included in the set of working drawings are a site plan, foundation plan, floor plans, exterior elevations, sections, and details. Also included are specifications, a written document spelling out the scope of the work to be performed and the methods and materials to be used. Together with the working drawings, the specifications become part of the construction contract. (The architect will make copies of the drawings for you, your builder, and any contractors—but retains ownership of the originals.)

You pay the final 20 percent of the fee when construction is complete.

PASSIVE SOLAR SYSTEMS: DIRECT GAIN

Warm, sun-drenched living spaces are the hallmark of a *direct-gain* passive solar heating system. Direct gain is the least complex of all passive systems, and the least expensive. Large south-facing windows bring sunshine into most rooms, creating an immediate surge of heat. Some of that heat—usually about one-third—is stored in the structure of the house and released later in the day as the sun sets and interiors begin to cool.

Despite the system's outward simplicity, direct gain requires precise balancing of its three major components. Its collectors—the south-facing windows—must be sized to admit just enough of the sun's energy to keep the house at a comfortable temperature at night.

Its storage mass—masonry, water, or containers of special chemical compounds—must be just large enough to absorb the required fraction of the day's solar harvest. Finally, its controls—insulation, summer shading, and vents—must have the proper design to prevent overheating in summer. (For more about this see pages 54-57 and 134-137.)

Striking a balance
If any of these three elements —collectors, heat storage, and controls—is improperly designed, the results will be hard to live with. The most common problem with poorly designed direct-gain systems is temperature fluctuation. During the day, living spaces may overheat; at night, the furnace may have trouble replacing heat lost through oversized windows. Fortunately, plenty of validated research is available to architects and engineers to assist them in designing even-tempered direct-gain systems.

As a homeowner, your responsibility is to understand the requirements and limitations of the system. Your needs are the designer's first priority, of course, but when modifying a design you'll have to be very careful about requesting major changes that might upset the balance of the system's major components.

The house shown here is a good example of thinking that helps shape a direct-gain house. Your house need not look like this one, but it will have to share certain features.

The most important feature is the location of living spaces.

Active living spaces—the living room, dining room, and family room—should be on the south side of the house where they will benefit directly from the sun's warmth. Heat-producing spaces—bathrooms, kitchen, and utility areas—should be to the north side of the house so their warmth can balance the sun-generated heat.

Orienting windows
Window sizes and placement are also critical, and can't be changed without careful consideration of the results. North-facing windows, which lose heat rapidly in winter, should

be kept to a minimum. West-facing and, to a lesser extent, east-facing windows gain a lot of heat in summer and are difficult to shade completely. Don't go overboard with glass on these faces of the house unless your area doesn't require air conditioning. Examine the schematic drawing and exterior view here and you'll see how almost the entire south side of this house opens up to receive sunlight.

Changing the location of interior partitions isn't a problem unless they are to act as storage masses. Masonry or water-filled walls need to be in a location where they are washed with sunlight throughout most of the day. If your home has a heat-storing floor, you can't cover it up with wall-to-wall carpeting and expect it to store much heat. A few small area rugs won't affect solar performance unreasonably, however.

Finally, don't ask for dramatic changes in any devices designed to shade south-facing windows in summer. These overhangs prevent overheating as the sun's arc becomes higher in the warmer seasons. Movable insulation under the skylight, *opposite,* also helps minimize summertime gains.

A direct-gain system also requires that you pay attention to certain details. The most important is covering windows at night with insulation to keep your precious solar heat inside. By learning to work with your home's solar system, you'll enjoy the lowest energy bills possible.

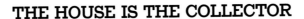

THE HOUSE IS THE COLLECTOR

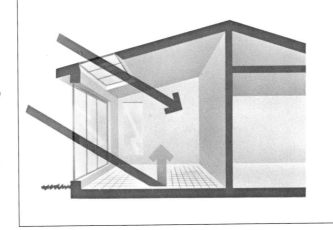

PASSIVE SOLAR SYSTEMS: INDIRECT GAIN

Although almost everyone enjoys living in a sunny house, too much sunlight can create headaches—literally. When one side of a room is far brighter than another side, a bad glare results.

Enter the *indirect-gain* system. As the exterior view of our example, *below,* shows, glass covers the house's south side, but inside, *opposite,* you'd never know it. That's because most of that glass is used only for collecting solar heat; a limited amount is reserved for the view.

Here's how an indirect system works: A few inches behind the collector glass is a storage wall, the most common of which is a Trombe wall. Named after its French inventor, Felix Trombe, the Trombe wall is a masonry structure 8 to 16 inches thick. Because the air space between the outside face of the wall and the collector glass is sealed, the wall's surface gets very hot on sunny days. The masonry absorbs most of this heat. As the day progresses, the heat works its way through the wall; by nightfall, the interior surface of the Trombe wall is comfortably warm. That warmth works through the wall by conduction, as illustrated in the drawing *at left.*

Don't get the idea, however, that a Trombe wall is a big chunk of concrete blocking the light and view: Windows are almost always included in the wall. In fact, the only clue that the wall is different from other walls is the deep "sill" below the windows. In the Trombe wall, *opposite,* the open glass areas also take care of heat needs during the day through direct gain. If your home requires still more heat during the day, add vents in the Trombe wall to allow warm air to circulate from the air space into the house via convection.

Through thick and thin

In addition to masonry Trombe walls, an indirect system can also use water- or chemical-filled walls to serve the same purpose. The most crucial design aspect of an indirect-gain system is the thickness of the storage wall. The Trombe wall pictured is 16 inches thick—just right for the heating needs of this home in New Mexico. If it is too thin, the wall, instead of storing most of the heat, will radiate too much heat into the house too quickly. If the wall is too thick, the solar heat won't make its way into the house until too late in the day.

Other elements of an indirect-gain system follow the pattern set by a direct-gain system. Again, living spaces should be on the south side of the house. It is also important that they be fairly shallow. The radiant heat from the storage wall has much less effect when you are more than about 20 feet from it.

Sun control is also very important in indirect-gain

systems. The surface of the collector wall will get very hot in summer if left unshaded; so hot, in fact, that the materials used in its construction might degrade over time. For this reason, most systems provide outside vents to exhaust the air space in summer.

You'll find it a bit easier to arrange furniture in a room with a Trombe wall than in a direct-gain room. Although you shouldn't back furnishings right up against a Trombe wall, you'll have more flexibility in your arrangement since you won't be faced with a wall of solid glass. The purpose of a Trombe wall is to radiate heat, so you won't want to adorn it with anything large and solid that would block the movement of heat; neither is it the place to hang fine artwork that the high wall temperatures may damage.

Cutting losses

Nighttime insulation is a must in very cold regions. This insulation must go on the outside of the storage wall, leaving the inside face free to radiate its heat. Because the air space is virtually inaccessible, such placement requires some form of remotely controlled insulation. You can also use manually controlled insulation mounted outside the collector glass, but this may require going outside in the evening to button-up the house.

Although the privacy provided by a Trombe wall is an advantage over direct-gain systems, the wall has one aesthetic drawback. For maximum efficiency, the outside face of the storage wall should be painted black or a very dark color. Some people don't like this, but from normal viewing distances the visual effect is minimal.

HOW A TROMBE WALL WORKS

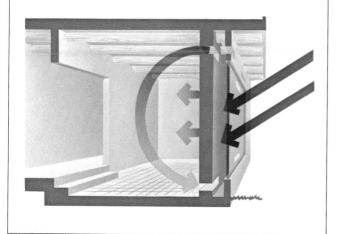

PASSIVE SOLAR SYSTEMS: ISOLATED GAIN

A SUNSPACE COLLECTS AND DISTRIBUTES HEAT

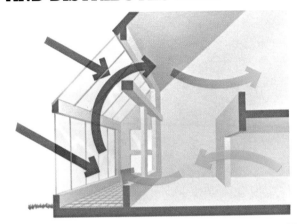

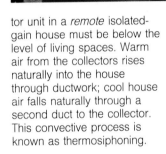

Controlling the flow of heat into living spaces is difficult with direct-gain passive solar systems. That's because the living space is the collection system. Heat in an *isolated-gain* system is collected away from living spaces, and you can control its movement.

The simplest isolated-gain system uses a sunspace—a south-facing room that serves as a walk-in solar collector (see Chapter 4). You open or close doors or vents between the sunspace and living spaces to regulate heat flow.

The house shown here collects heat in twin greenhouses facing south, *opposite*. Windows between the greenhouse and living spaces are opened when heat is needed, *above right*. This warm air then flows up to the second floor, and back down to the main level through vents in the floor. The drawing *above* shows the basic flow of heated air through the house. This ability to control heat flow—and to prevent overheating—is the most appealing feature of isolated-gain systems.

Sunspaces used this way are unsuitable as year-round living areas. For maximum efficiency, the sunspace must become very warm during the day and very cool at night. Temperature swings from 95 degrees Fahrenheit down to 40 degrees are typical in cold climates or where freezing occurs occasionally.

A big plus for the isolated-gain system is that the house's main living spaces need not face south. Small fans can move air from the sunspace to any part of the house needing heat. Still, many houses with sunspaces have living spaces along the south side of the house. This enables the homeowners to view and enjoy the sunspace.

Another way to go

Another form of isolated-gain heating (often called the *thermosiphon* system) puts a collector unit away from the house and below most living spaces. In these designs, the collector is similar to those used in active air heating systems (see page 90). But unlike active air systems, the collec-

tor unit in a *remote* isolated-gain house must be below the level of living spaces. Warm air from the collectors rises naturally into the house through ductwork; cool house air falls naturally through a second duct to the collector. This convective process is known as thermosiphoning.

Storing heat

Isolated-gain systems require heat storage. In a sunspace scheme, storage often is built into the walls and floor, or added in the form of water-filled containers or phase-change materials. In effect, the sunspace is a modified version of a simple direct-gain system.

If the sunspace is so large that it collects a great deal of excess heat, remote storage areas (in the basement, for example) also may be added. Generally consisting of a large, insulated, rock-filled bin or a box filled with containers of water, remote storage areas must be planned carefully. If the storage bin is directly under the floor of living spaces, heat can rise naturally through vents or by radiation

through a masonry floor into living areas. If the remote storage isn't next to living spaces, the warmth must flow to the spaces via ductwork (often the same ductwork used to move furnace-heated air).

What about costs?

The cost of an isolated-gain system is usually somewhat higher than either a direct-gain or an indirect-gain system, primarily because you are adding square footage to the house that is unusable for living every day of the year. But don't let the extreme temperature swings rule out stocking the sunspace with living things; many plants can take the swings, and many owners of sunspace-equipped houses enjoy this bonus greenhouse space. Some even grow a variety of vegetables for winter use (more about this on pages 122-129). For this reason and because they're delightful retreats during the times of the year when they can be used as living space, isolated-gain systems with sunspaces are among the most popular of the passive solar heating designs.

PASSIVE SOLAR SYSTEMS: ENVELOPE HOUSES

ANATOMY OF AN ENVELOPE HOUSE

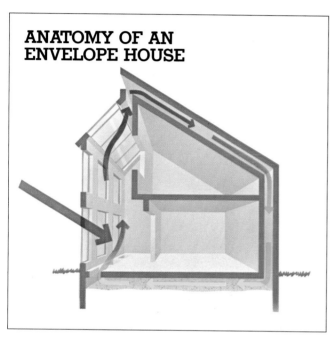

Think of the envelope system as a house within a house—one that has an air space between the roof and ceiling, and also between inner and outer walls on the north side.

The illustration *at left* shows how this design works. Sun heats air in a south-facing greenhouse. Warm air rises to the air space up top, known as a *plenum*. There, convection circulates the air in a loop across the ceiling and down the north wall, blanketing the home's two biggest heat-losing surfaces with what amounts to solar insulation. Finally, the air enters a crawl space under the floor of the house and flows back up into the greenhouse through vents.

The extra insulation allowed by the double shell, along with the airtightness of the house, makes these homes extremely energy efficient. (Some solar authorities argue that these two factors account for most of the efficiency. They say you could achieve much the same results by keeping the insulation levels high and eliminating the plenums altogether.)

Regardless of why it's energy efficient, the envelope design has worked well in climates ranging from the Sun Belt to the Canadian border. In many cases if extra heat is required, the owners merely stoke up a wood stove to take off the chill. Of course in most temperate climates, you'll need a complete backup heating system. Electric room heaters are one possibility. As in any airtight home, you'd be wise to plan for forced ventilation of fresh air. (Refer to pages 44 and 45 to learn about providing ventilation for a tight home.)

Living in an envelope

Check the photo *opposite* and you can see one major benefit of an envelope home: its two-story-high sunspace. Owners report that theirs stay warm enough all year round for most houseplants, even if no extra heat is supplied. Another benefit of the system is that virtually any style of house can be adapted to it. As you can see from the exterior view *at lower left,* it works very well with contemporary styling, and envelopes have blended successfully into Cape Cod designs as well.

Room placement within envelope houses is unrestricted, but most plans call for living spaces to the south, where they can pick up warm air from the greenhouse. Heat-producing areas, such as kitchens, bathrooms, and laundries, often go at the north side of the house.

The design of an envelope house requires careful attention to many details. In some communities, the large, open plenums are considered fire hazards. In a fire, the plenum could act as a chimney, carrying flames around the structure. That's why most envelope houses include special heat-sensitive dampers that seal off the plenums if the temperature becomes too high.

Envelope homes are a new concept, and few builders have experience with them. However, some communities have architects and builders who specialize in this type of home. If you cannot find one in your area, check the advertising in home-building magazines for firms that sell plans for envelope homes by mail order. These companies can help you find a builder qualified to produce a home of this type.

PASSIVE COOLING SYSTEMS

Although passive heating gets most of the attention, passive cooling is just as important to millions of homeowners. The most important design strategy is to prevent heat buildup in the first place. Insulation should be your first line of defense. Insulation keeps heat outside just as effectively in summer as it keeps it inside in winter.

In climates where cooling costs exceed heating costs, windows should be placed to minimize solar gain in summer. Large glass areas can face north, but east and west windows should be minimized unless they're shaded. And south windows, which may be necessary for some winter heating, must have broad overhangs.

The second important cooling strategy is shading. Deciduous shade trees on the south and west sides of the house will help cool your home in summer, then conveniently drop their leaves in winter to allow sunlight to enter the house.

If mature shade trees are unavailable, overhangs can provide cooling shade too. The photographs *at left* illustrate how overhangs work. In summer, *above,* the sun travels high in the sky. The overhang keeps the direct rays of the sun off south-facing glass areas. In winter, *below,* the sun moves in a lower arc and its rays can sneak in under the overhangs.

In summer, even an overhang won't provide much protection against early-morning sun on east windows and, especially, late-afternoon sun on west windows. For these, awnings and sunshades, such as those shown on pages 134-137, work better. Adjustable awnings are also effective on south windows because they

can block the sun on warm spring and fall days when the sun is too low in the sky for fixed overhangs to keep out.

Improved ventilation

Insulation and shading devices can greatly reduce the need for air conditioning, but they aren't totally effective against long spells of hot weather. A second design strategy—ventilation—can help take up the slack. Ventilation serves two important functions. First, it exhausts the heat that builds up within the house because of daily living activities such as cooking, laundering, and bathing. Second, it creates airflow, which reduces the perceived temperature. Sitting in the breeze of a fan is the most common example of how moving air feels cooler. With proper ventilation, you can reduce the need to move air mechanically. Still, fans are a good idea—particularly whole-house fans that move massive amounts of air. (For more about upgrading ventilation, see pages 44 and 45.)

Positioning windows to take advantage of natural breezes and cross ventilation is an excellent start. In some parts of the country—particularly arid, windless regions—a thermal chimney might make sense. In the house shown *above,* the

tall stack on the right side of the house has plastic glazing on its south side. As the sun warms the air inside the stack, it rises to the top of the stack and exits through the louvered vent. Openings between the stack and living spaces allow house air to move into the stack, creating a gentle breeze. (For more about thermal chimneys, see page 57.)

A variation on this theme is the earth-tube concept. Replacement air is drawn into the house through long tubes running underground. The soil around the tubes cools the air before it gets into the house. (You also can learn more about earth tubes on page 57.)

The problem with all of these passive cooling systems is that they can't reduce the humidity of incoming air to a comfortable level. If you're designing a new house from scratch, you have a *better* opportunity to address cooling problems than you might in a retrofit situation. However, no known passive cooling system will provide comfort as reliably as "old-fashioned" electrical air conditioning. The best answer to cooling problems seems to lie in *reducing* the need for ordinary air conditioning, so you have to turn it on only in the hottest, stickiest weather.

ACTIVE HEATING SYSTEMS

Planning a house to use active solar components is little different from planning a conventional home. Active systems are mechanical add-ons, not unlike a furnace or central air conditioning system.

You can make installation of an active system easier by using a little forethought. Sloping a roof at the correct angle for solar collection at your latitude will make mounting the collectors simpler. (Your system designer can best determine the proper slope.) You also should make certain that room exists for ductwork, pipes, and electrical runs between the collectors and the utility room. Finally, plan for the extra space needed to house the special equipment that comes with the system you purchase.

Active air systems
The photograph *above* shows how sound planning allows an active air system to blend in with the house. In an air-type system, the collectors circulate house air over glass-covered black plates. In this case, the collectors are tucked in between regular roof rafters.

The sun-warmed air can heat the house directly, or its warmth can be stored in a water-filled tank or in an insulated box of rocks. An active air heating system can also be used to heat domestic hot water; more about this on page 90. The major benefit of an air system is that it can't freeze up in cold weather. But because air is a less efficient way of transporting heat, the collectors must be larger than those used in the other major active system, the active liquid system.

Liquid systems
Liquid-type systems circulate a fluid—usually antifreeze and water—through a flat black, glass-covered plate. A pump then forces the heated solution into a storage tank. A radiator-like heat exchanger picks up heat from the tank, and ducts warm air to the home's normal heating system ducts.

The photograph *at right* shows how the collectors can mount directly on a properly sloped roof. If no suitable roof space is available, both liquid and air collectors can go on the ground.

Solar-assisted heat pumps
A hybrid active system is the solar-assisted heat pump. As with all heat pumps, this type works like an air conditioner that runs in reverse for winter heating. The heat pump's coils are mounted in full sun so they can absorb solar heat and transfer it into the house. In summer, a second, different set of outside coils radiates away the heat picked up inside the house.

A similar heat-pump system uses ground water instead of the sun to supply heat to the coils. Since ground water receives its heat from the sun-warmed earth, this system can rightly be considered solar-assisted. Ground-water heat pumps also use water to absorb heat from the coils in summer. A special well and drainage system are needed for ground-water heat pumps, so be sure to consult a qualified engineer before purchasing one.

All active systems require precise engineering and sizing. Even most architects defer to engineers when it comes to active solar heating. Be sure to get authoritative help when considering any active system.

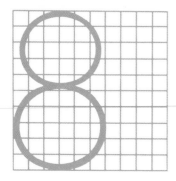

SOLAR DECORATING BASICS

What's special about decorating a solar home? If it is heated by an active or an indirect-gain system, the answer is "very little." But direct-gain houses—and any room designed to capture and hold the sun's heat—need to stand up to its awesome energy and use that energy efficiently. Whether you're designing and building a new solar home or adding solar capability to an older one, here's what you need to know about the sunny side of decorating.

When you invite the sun into your home, you have to take the bad along with the good. All that solar heat and natural light can pose some decorating limitations. Only a few materials can resist sun damage. In the family room *opposite*, woven wicker, reflective white cushions, a wood-and-cane rocking chair, and wood-and-rush dining chairs all can withstand a lot of heat and sunlight. Other good choices are chrome and glass, or wood- or steel-framed pieces with replaceable cushions. Upholstered pieces are less practical because, unless they're made of highly resistant materials, they'll deteriorate quickly. (The following pages tell about selecting fabrics.)

Furniture size and arrangement are important

When selecting furniture, keep in mind that large-scale pieces may shade and block thermal mass, restricting the amount of heat it can capture. Also, bulky pieces impede airflow and heat distribution. Small-scale, open-back, open-arm pieces, and furniture that is open underneath help thermal mass do its best work.

In many direct-gain rooms, the floor is part of the thermal mass and, to do its job properly, should remain uncovered. If you want to use a rug, choose a small one you can remove during the day, or opt for small, open-weave, natural-fiber rugs (such as sisal or rush matting) that won't greatly restrict the flow of heat into and out of the floor mass.

How you arrange furniture also affects comfort and energy efficiency. As pictured *opposite*, seating should be arranged so no one has to face directly into the sun. Also, nothing tall should go in front of windows. In this room, a tall hutch stands in a shady corner, where it hides from the sun's strongest rays and doesn't block incoming light.

Art and accessories

A direct-gain solar room, with its bright light, high heat, and high humidity, is not a sensible place to display fine artwork. Sunlight can crack oil pigments and damage paper works. Watercolors will begin to fade in a very short time; acrylics are somewhat more sun resistant, but still find a sun-filled room an unfriendly habitat. Display prized artwork in north-facing rooms or in shady hallways and stairwells.

Although sunlight damages some forms of art, it can enhance others. A stained glass window can bring non-fading color to your room. Or consider strategically placing sculpture, mobiles, and large plants to cast interesting shadows that change with the hours.

Color and pattern are welcome in a sun-filled space, but choose accessories that you won't be heartbroken about replacing if the colors fade. Tablecloths and throw pillows in bright, inexpensive cotton prints fill the bill, as do baskets, inexpensive posters, and dried flowers.

WHICH FABRICS
STAND UP
TO THE SUN?

When you're choosing fabrics for a sunspace, you have to consider not only visual appeal and physical comfort, but also what will happen to the fabrics after long exposure to sunlight. In the room shown *opposite* the owners selected a muted stripe that will remain attractive even if the colors fade.

With time, almost any color will fade to some degree, but neutrals and earth tones fade less noticeably than do brighter hues. Dyes for earth tones are more likely to come from natural sources, and less likely to bleach out than synthetic dyes.

Intense sunlight can cause fibers to deteriorate as well as fade. Fabrics with the tightest weaves will hold their own better than those with loose weaves, which allow for more stretching and weakening of the fibers.

High humidity can shorten a fabric's life, also. Materials that are highly absorbent tend to stretch as they soak up moisture, losing strength and resiliency. For seating pieces, upholstery fabric should be only slightly absorbent—just enough to ensure comfort.

Fabrics manufactured specifically for upholstery—those made of acrylic, cotton, linen, leather, nylon, polyester, and wool—are likely to be the most durable, with sturdy weaves and sun-resistant dyes. Avoid materials designed for other purposes.

Fabric window treatments have to withstand large temperature swings, condensation, and light, without losing their shape. Acrylic, modacrylic, glass fiber, nylon, and polyester are good fade-, heat-, and moisture-resistant choices. The chart *at right* can help you evaluate which fibers will work best in a solar room.

CHOOSING FABRICS FOR SUNSPACES

FIBER NAME	EFFECT OF SUNLIGHT	RESISTANCE TO HEAT	MOISTURE ABSORBENCY
NATURAL			
COTTON	Gradual yellowing and loss of strength	Excellent heat resistance	Medium
LEATHER	No loss of strength; slight discoloration	Becomes brittle without proper care	Low
LINEN	Gradual loss of strength	Discolors at high temperature	High
SILK	Moderate loss of strength	Less affected than wool	Medium
WOOL	Loss of strength; gradual fading	Loses softness from prolonged exposure to sun	High
SYNTHETIC			
ACETATE	Slight loss of strength; little color loss	Little degradation	Low
ACRYLIC	Very little loss of strength; no discoloration	Little degradation	Low
GLASS FIBER	Very little deterioration in strength or color	Very resistant to heat	Low
NYLON	Gradual loss of strength; little loss of color	Little degradation	Low
POLYESTER	Very gradual loss of strength; no discoloration	Little degradation	Low
RAYON	Gradual loss of strength	Little degradation	High
VINYL	No loss of strength; little discoloration	Gradually becomes brittle	Non-absorbent

LIVING WITH THERMAL MASS

Gone are the days when "thermal mass" meant only black-painted drums of water lining south-facing windows. Today thermal mass can—and should—be an attractive, integral part of a solar home's design. And because all surfaces in a room radiate heat to one another, thermal mass needn't face directly south.

Storing in style
The sunspace *opposite* includes a handsome tile floor and built-in water tanks for maximum heat storage capac-

ity. If you cannot find the tanks, look again; they are the textured plant ledges at the left. The tanks extend into both the sunspace and the adjacent living areas so that heat soaked up on one side transfers to the other.

The more irregular the surface material, the more surface area exposed to the sun— and this means greater heat absorption. These tanks, stuccoed and painted a warm terra-cotta tone to match the tile floor, are highly absorbent and also add decorative texture to the room.

Hot seats
In the living room *below* the inviting window seat conceals a series of water-filled tanks that help store solar heat from the south-facing window wall. Thermal mass seating needn't be built-in, either. You can select sofas with hollow bases that conceal water tanks for heat storage. Storage tanks also can hide decoratively behind facades that look like bookcases or cabinets.

Masonry mass walls
Your best choice for a masonry wall is a material you really

love. That way you won't feel compelled to cover it with anything else. For example, a brick or adobe wall looks great all by itself and can add welcome texture to an otherwise plain, smooth-walled home. At night, an inexpensive uplight on the floor angled to the side of or below a rough brick or stone wall will throw the materials into sharp relief for even more textural drama.

For decorative accents on a mass wall, try a few small objects (ceramic plates, baskets, metal items) or open-weave fiber wall hangings. For a touch of drama and softness, place a large tree, plant, or sculpture near the wall. Incoming daylight will create delightful shadow play, and a strategically placed canister light can do the same thing at night.

Variety underfoot
A mass floor can be made of any material that readily absorbs and conducts heat, such as quarry or concrete tile, slate, brick, or other natural ceramic material.

In the living room *at left* a heat-retaining concrete slab floor becomes a decorative asset. The concrete was stained a mellow gray-brown before it was poured. Then it received a protective coat of satiny wax. Far from appearing cold and industrial, a concrete floor like this has the warmth and character of aged stone— at a fraction of the cost.

Another unusual decorative option is a poured-aggregate floor that adds the color variations of river-washed pebbles to ordinary concrete.

SAVING AND
SHADING WITH
WINDOW TREATMENTS

At night, uncovered windows let stored solar heat escape too fast for comfort; and during the day, especially in summer, a bare window can gain a lot of unwanted heat. Solar-effective window treatments address both problems.

To conserve heat, a window treatment must satisfy certain criteria. It must cover the window with insulating material that minimizes radiation through the glass. Also, the treatment should seal tightly to the window's frame. This keeps out drafts and prevents warm room air from getting between the covering and the glass, where it can condense. Energy-efficient window coverings should have a moisture barrier to help reduce condensation, and a reflective surface to deflect summer heat.

In some solar rooms, you also may want a treatment that lets in light but controls glare—a sheer drapery panel or curtain, or horizontal or vertical slat blinds. However, use these alternatives only in combination with another energy-efficient window treatment.

Sealing with shades

In the bedroom *opposite* a dark-green shade (which matches the water-filled storage wall) greatly reduces heat losses. The shade, made with a kit available from fabric stores, has an insulating lining and magnetic edging that secures it to the window's metal frame. A valance corks the top against heat loss and drafts. The shade pulls up, Roman-style, to admit maximum light during the day.

Another ready-made tailored style is a quilted roll-up shade, shown *at upper right*. It seals with magnetic tape sewn into the edges and tacked or glued to the window frame.

The romantic ready-made balloon shade, *lower right,* has a hidden layer of insulation. A natural for wooden windows where magnets won't work, its edges seal tightly by snapping into plastic glides attached to the window trim.

Other options

Shades aren't the only way to control energy gains and losses. In Chapter 3, we suggested insulated shutters. Here are other decorative choices:
● *Drapery liners.* If draperies or curtains suit your decorating style, you can help them hold in heat by layering an insulating liner behind them. A liner with a reflective surface will also fend off summer heat.
● *Window mat.* This unobtrusive insulator provides another way to enjoy the look of traditional window treatments without sacrificing efficiency. The mat is a layered "sandwich" of insulating material, vapor barrier, and decorative fabric, which seals to the window trim with magnetic tape. During the day, you can remove the mat and roll it up as a bolster. For more about making a window mat, see pages 144 and 145.
● *Rigid pop-in panels.* Made from sheets of foil-faced fiber glass, pop-in panels fit snugly inside window frames at night, and double as decorative wall hangings during the day. Pages 140 and 141 give detailed instructions about how to make them.
● *Sliding panels.* If you prefer movable insulation that stays in the window during the day, sliding panels offer an alternative. Hung from a ceiling track, two panels cover the window at night, and slide behind decorative fixed side panels to let the sun in. To see how the panels look, and how to make them, see pages 142 and 143.

PUTTING ROOMS
IN THE
RIGHT LIGHT

One guideline applies to creating inviting, appealing lighting and to saving energy: *Put the light only where you need it.* Flooding every nook and cranny with light not only wastes precious energy, it also results in a stark, shadowless space that's boring to the eye. So, aim for an interplay of light and shadow.

In terms of actual energy consumption, incandescent lighting, although traditionally the most appealing because of its warm glow, is the least efficient form of lighting. When buying bulbs, look for energy-saving types with a higher lumen-per-watt ratio than ordinary bulbs have; also consider reflector bulbs to reduce wasteful light spill.

Fluorescent lighting is about three times more efficient than incandescent is and, thus, is less costly to operate. (For information about choosing fluorescent lighting, see the box *at right.*)

For accent lighting, consider low-voltage track modules and recessed lighting, which use 6 or 12 volts of electricity, instead of the usual 120 volts.

In this family room, *left,* fluorescent and incandescent lighting work well together. Warm-tone fluorescent tubes provide an energy-saving wash of illumination along a windowless wall. The tubes were built into three-sided columns to shield them from direct view. Adjustable canister lights spotlight the dining area and uplight items on the glass coffee table. Portable gooseneck lamps fill in with additional accent and task lighting when it's needed.

You may want to take upholstery and paint samples with you when you shop for lighting to see how their colors will appear.

CHOOSING FLUORESCENT LIGHTING

If you want to dispel the dark economically, fluorescent lighting is the way to go, and no longer do you have to settle for a cold, industrial atmosphere. Different fluorescent tubes satisfy different lighting needs. To find the light that's right for you consider these three factors.

• The *lumen-per-watt ratio* tells you how many units of light you'll get for each watt of electricity used. The higher the number, the more efficient the lighting source. However, lumens tell you nothing about the *quality* of light a tube casts.

• The *C.R.I. (color rendering index)* can help you judge the way a light source shows colors. This lighting industry standard is denoted by an R factor, with an R of 100 the standard reference point. You can think of it as indicating the way colors appear in daylight. The closer the R factor is to 100, the more truly the light source renders colors.

• *Degrees Kelvin (K)* tells about the appearance of the light itself. This rating is a theoretical measure of color temperature, but K measurements are opposite to our everyday perception of colors. The "warm" shades have a *lower* K than the "cool" shades. The K rating of a fluorescent lamp won't tell you how hot it gets, but it will give you an idea of how the light looks. Thus, a "warm-tone" fluorescent tube would have a *lower* K than a "cool," bluer-toned fluorescent.

You'll probably prefer warm-toned light where you want a low level of illumination and a cozy, relaxed atmosphere. Warm fluorescents flatter skin tones and blend well with incandescents, as in the room *at left.* Cool-toned light creates a sharp, businesslike atmosphere. If your home has an artist or hobbyist who needs to see color accurately, choose fluorescent lamps that have a high R factor and a high K temperature. The light they give off will appear cool, and colors will seem vivid and sharp.

If you'd like your indoor lighting to be as close to sunlight as possible, you may want to consider fluorescent tubes referred to as "full-spectrum" or as "simulating sunlight." The distribution of colors and ultraviolet in the light they produce is very similar to that of daylight. Under this lighting, colors will appear as they do in daylight, with almost no distortion. This lighting is excellent for any close or detail work, and some researchers report improvements in concentration and visual acuity. Others say that full-spectrum fluorescent lighting provides certain health benefits—increasing the rate of calcium absorption, reducing cavities, and reducing disruptive behavior in school children. These findings are considered controversial, however, and scientists are still doing further research.

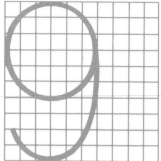

GROWING FOOD ALL YEAR ROUND

Don't hang up your hoe just because cold weather is approaching; with solar assistance, you can extend the growing season to a full year. Whether you incorporate a vegetable garden into a sunspace or simply use cold frames and cloches, the solar strategy is the same: Protect your plants from the cold, while giving them light and warmth from the sun.

When you first think about it, a sunspace may seem a natural place to grow food. After all, can't you use the same sunlight that helps heat your home to also nourish plants? The answer is yes and no. A sunspace, you'll recall, works most efficiently with a minimum of glazing on the roof and sidewalls. A greenhouse, on the other hand, needs to provide plants with maximum sunlight at all times of year; if you want to grow food, the more glass, the better the results.

A sunspace can, however, help you stretch the growing season far into winter and hail the arrival of spring well ahead of the calendar.

Starting flowers and vegetables from seed is one way you can put your sunspace to work. In the solarium shown on these two pages, flats of vegetable starts are almost ready to be transplanted to the garden. The raised growing beds are sized to fit commercial window-box liners and growing flats. This makes it easy to shift around the flats of

plants or, when you want, to transport them to the garden.

Also, growing conditions vary perceptibly throughout this sunspace's vertical environment. Some plants thrive in the upper beds; others fare better closer to the floor. The movable plant boxes allow the owners to give each plant the conditions that it likes best.

In autumn, garden plants can go back into the sunspace where they'll continue to produce long after outside gardens are snow covered. In this sunspace, for example, tomato plants go right on producing each year until December. In the same way, annuals will continue to flower when taken indoors.

When transplanting flowers or vegetables, you can pot them in containers, as the owners did with the plants shown here, or plant them in soil-filled growing beds. Before bringing them inside, however, be sure to isolate all plants for a few days, then check for pests. This will help protect your plants that remain indoors all year long.

PRODUCING FOOD IN YOUR SUNSPACE

You can grow nearly any food under the sun in a greenhouse; but doing it correctly means understanding the ins and outs of indoor gardening. One example: Sunlight is unevenly scattered throughout most greenhouses. To cultivate vegetables, you need to know how much light each needs and then give it its proper place in the sun.

Anyone can become an indoor green-thumber. All that is required is genuine care for growing things and adherence to the following advice.

Size up the situation

Look for ways to use every available inch in the sunspace. Don't overdo it, however. Leave enough room to move about easily, and take care not to block the sun from crops that require a lot of light. Also, use a variety of containers and configurations for planting. That way, you can grow a diverse range of crops.

Treat them right

Plants need great quantities of carbon dioxide. During the winter, they may not get enough. Mulching will help.

An adequate flow of air is essential. Natural ventilation is least expensive, but you may need a fan if the sunspace is tightly sealed. Moreover, if the greenhouse becomes too humid, increase the ventilation, and water early in the morning.

Although a greenhouse shields plants from the full effect of the outdoor climate, its interior climate still changes with the seasons. For maximum food production, monitor your greenhouse climate and seasonal changes so you can plant the right crops at the right time. For example, cool-weather vegetables, such as salad greens and root crops, thrive when temperatures within the greenhouse drop. Then in summer, as temperatures within the greenhouse rise, plants such as tomatoes, egg-plant, and cucumbers grow well. (For more about cool- and warm-weather crops, see page 126 and the chart on pages 128 and 129.)

Be aware of the growing conditions in your greenhouse, and place the crops accordingly. Keep in mind that temperatures are coolest near the ground. In summer, put crops near south glazing only if they need a lot of light and can take the heat. In winter, locations near glazing will be the coldest nighttime spots. Vegetables on the north wall will get the most sun in winter and the least in summer. Also, place crops that can't tolerate temperature swings near the thermal mass.

Sow, and you shall reap

Sow cool-weather crops when temperatures inside the green-house are about 50 degrees F at night and 60 degrees F during the day. Don't start them, however, if temperatures go above 77 degrees F.

Sow warm-weather vegeta-bles when greenhouse temperatures are about 65 degrees F at night and up to 90 degrees F in the daytime. In any event, don't allow greenhouse temperatures to stay in the high 80s for long: Your plants won't survive. Be sure not to start seedlings you will move outdoors until six weeks before the frost-free date.

The sunspace shown on these two pages is a visual delight. The owners couldn't add on downstairs, so they used space on the second floor, going out from the master bedroom, *opposite, above.* Before, the room ended at the low back beam where the thermometer now hangs, *opposite, below.* The expansion makes for a more pleasant bedroom, as well as a food-producing greenhouse, complete with vegetable starts in cold frames, *below.*

(continued)

RAISING FISH IN A SUNSPACE

Ever think about starting a fish farm? A sunspace like the one shown *below* makes an ideal place to raise fish for your table.

Tilapia, the variety of fish shown here, grows well in a solar environment because it feeds primarily on algae produced when sunlight hits the tank.

A fiber glass tank 5 feet high and 2 to 5 feet in diameter is a good choice. Add water, but wait at least 24 hours before putting in the fish. (Purchase them when they are 1 to 2 inches long.) Caring for Tilapia is easy. Just supplement the algae with dried trout food, and make sure the temperature in the sunspace stays above 53 degrees F.

After three or four months—when Tilapia are ¼ to ½ pound and about 8 inches long—you're ready to begin one of the tastiest harvests you'll ever make. Tilapia—a firm white fish, similar in taste to cod or haddock—is delicious either sautéed or poached.

PRODUCING FOOD IN YOUR SUNSPACE
(continued)

The greenhouse pictured here started life strictly as a growing space. Now it's also a sunspace, saving money on energy as well as on food. The original single-glazed panels were made more efficient by adding acrylic storm windows. A soil floor and flagstone path, *lower right*, provide some thermal mass, and the family plans to add more in the form of water-filled containers, canisters of phase-change materials, or a new concrete slab floor. Sliding glass doors between the greenhouse and the family room control heat flow into the living area.

Soil and water
Whether you plan your sunspace greenhouse from scratch or convert an existing one, you need to provide the right growing medium for your crops. A good, tried-and-true soil mix is one part each of rich organic topsoil, compost or peat, and vermiculite or perlite.

Soil that's constantly in use needs nutrients between plantings. To supply them naturally, either add organic matter to the soil or rotate the crops. If you use commercial fertilizers, buy those that fulfill specific needs.

Start cool-weather crops in 2-inch-deep flats. Five or six hours of daily sunlight will give your seedlings a good start in life. When the second true set of leaves appears, transplant the seedlings into greenhouse beds. (Winter beds should be deep so the soil mass can help insulate the plants.) Water at least every two to three days, and only in the morning to prevent disease caused by soil that stays damp overnight.

Plant warm-weather crops in the same manner as cool-weather ones, but water them around noon, so the greenhouse will not become too hot in the afternoon. Cool the greenhouse by opening all vents and doors, setting up a fan, and spraying the floor with water. If you share living space with your vegetables, you may prefer to move your summer garden outdoors until the weather cools off.

Hydroponics
Soil is by far the most popular growing medium, but you have an alternative, known as "hydroponics." The idea here is to short-cut the complicated chemical exchanges that take place in ordinary soil and make the crucial nutrients directly available to plants. One way to do this is to set the plants into a soilless medium such as perlite, vermiculite, coarse sand, or gravel, and then add a specially prepared nutrient solution. Or, eliminate the medium and grow the plants by suspending the roots in the nutrient solution.

One advantage hydroponics offers indoor gardeners is that the system takes up less space than conventional growing techniques. For example, you can grow a 6-foot tomato vine in a small pot. Another advantage is that you minimize the risk of soil-borne diseases.

Hydroponic systems can be as simple as an ordinary flowerpot filled with vermiculite through which you pour a cup of nutrient solution once or twice a day. Or, you can invest in elaborate automatic setups with pumps, timers, valves, and other devices.

GREENHOUSE GARDENER'S GUIDE

GREENHOUSE GARDENING BASICS

	SEEDING CONDITIONS	DAYS TILL GERMINATION	GROWING CONDITIONS
COOL-WEATHER CROPS			
Beets	½" to 1" deep; 2" apart; 65° F	7 to 10	Plant 2" apart; 40° to 70° F. Tolerate some shade.
Broccoli (sprouting)	½" deep; ½" apart; 60° F	3 to 10	Needs 18" to 24" all around; 40° to 65° F. Can't tolerate bright light.
Carrots	¼" deep; thin to 2" or 3" apart (varies with type); 60° to 80° F	10 to 17	Plant 2" or 3" apart; 45° to 65° F. Can tolerate some shade.
Cauliflower	½" deep; ½" apart; 60° F	4 to 10	Needs 18" all around; 40° to 60° F. Can't tolerate many bright days.
Chives	½" to 1" deep; 8 to 10 seeds per gallon of soil; 60° to 70° F	8 to 12	Plant 8" apart. Tolerate varying temperatures well, but minimum of 35° F. Like full sunlight.
Lettuce (head)	¼" to ½" apart; 4 to 8 seeds per gallon container; 60° to 75° F	4 to 10	Plant 4" apart, then transplant to 8" to 14" (varies with type); 45° to 60° F. Tolerates some shade.
Lettuce (leaf)	¼" to ½" apart; 8 to 12 seeds per gallon container; 60° to 75° F	4 to 10	Plant 4" to 6" apart; 45° to 60° F. Tolerates some shade.
Peas	2" deep; 15 seeds per gallon, then thin; 50° to 70° F	6 to 15	Plant 2" to 3" apart; 40° to 60° F. Can tolerate some shade.
Radishes	¼" to ½" deep; about 15 seeds per gallon; 60° to 80° F	3 to 10	Plant 1" to 2" apart; 55° to 65° F. Can tolerate some shade.
Spinach	½" deep; ½" apart; 60° to 80° F	10	Plant 6" apart; 40° to 50° F. Tolerates some shade.
WARM-WEATHER CROPS			
Beans (pole; bush)	2" deep; pole beans about 5" apart, bush beans 6" to 8" apart; 60° F soil	6 to 14	Plant pole beans 6" to 10" apart; bush beans 3" to 6" apart; 50° to 70° F. Like full sun.
Cucumbers	½" to 1" deep; 2" apart; 70° to 90° F	6 to 10	Plant from 12" to 36" apart (varies with size); 65° to 90° F, no cooler than 50° F. Like full sun.
Eggplant	¼" to ½" deep; 2" apart; 70° to 90° F	7 to 14	Leave 1½' to 2' all around; 65° to 75° F. Like full sun.
Peppers	¼" deep; 1" apart; 70° to 85° F	10 to 20	Plant from 12" to 24" apart (varies with type); 65° to 80° F. Like full sun.
Tomatoes	¼" to ½" deep; ½" to 1" apart; 65° to 80° F	6 to 14	Plant from 18" to 36" apart (varies with size); 65° to 80° F (poor growth above 95° and below 50° F). Like full sun.

TIME TILL HARVEST	COMMENTS
About 2 months	Prefer slightly alkaline soil (add lime or wood ash).
60 to 80 days (plus 5 to 7 weeks to grow to transplant size)	Not efficient since it takes up so much room—but tasty.
60 to 80 days	Prefer sandy soil; don't transplant.
50 to 70 days (plus 5 to 7 weeks to grow to transplant size)	Takes up a lot of room, but high grocery-store prices may justify use of space, especially in large greenhouses.
80 to 90 days, but may take more than one season to become a good producer	Cut back to 1″ and fertilize to stimulate winter growth.
50 to 80 days (plus 3 to 5 weeks to grow to transplant size)	Harvest entire plant or large leaves from the bottom; check heat tolerance of the variety you select.
45 to 60 days (plus 3 to 5 weeks to grow to transplant size)	Can take longer to mature in coldest months.
2 to 3 months	Vine varieties use vertical space; treat with bacterial inoculant. Check heat tolerance.
20 to 50 days	One of the easiest crops to grow.
60 to 70 days	Doesn't like the heat.
Pole: 3 to 4 months; bush: 1½ to 3 months	Pole beans take advantage of vertical space; bush beans work well in containers.
55 to 65 days (plus 4 weeks to grow to transplant size)	Need lots of water; mulch helps to prevent loss of nutrients and helps to maintain warm soil temperatures.
75 to 95 days (plus 6 to 9 weeks to grow to transplant size)	Long, thin varieties are typically easier to pollinate.
60 to 80 days (plus 6 to 8 weeks to grow to transplant size)	Dwarf varieties will save space.
55 to 90 days (plus 5 to 7 weeks to grow to transplant size)	Need hand pollination; come in bush and vine varieties; need plenty of potassium; cherry tomatoes particularly hardy.

COLD FRAMES AND COVER-UPS

Use the backyard greenhouse, shown *at left*, to start vegetables in pots or flats or plant them directly in the earth underneath. The 10x5-foot frame, which you can disassemble when not using it, is essentially a rectangle of 2x4s with a 5-foot upright at each end. A 3-inch galvanized pipe across the top completes the frame and provides the structure over which the "ribs"—1-inch PVC tubing—are positioned. Heavy plastic rests on the frame; you can secure it with grommets. To make rolling and unrolling the plastic easy, attach thin aluminum pipe to each side of the sheet.

Think of a cold frame as a very short greenhouse. Although smaller, it works exactly the same way. When the cold frame includes thermal mass, as the one *at left* does, you can use it year round to produce vegetables that would normally grow only in warm climates. In this commercially available cold frame, a 55-gallon drum, painted black and filled with water, provides the thermal mass. The curve in the double-glazed fiber glass top gives plants plenty of space to grow.

Whether you want a full-scale sunspace attached to your home, a mini-greenhouse for the backyard, or a smaller variation called a *cold frame*, the same solar principles apply. In every case, translucent material lets sunlight in but, at the same time, shields tender plants from the elements. In some units, thermal mass allows heat-loving vegetables to grow in the winter. Finally, movable or removable covers or lids provide ventilation.

The cold frame shown *at left* really doesn't need your help at all. An automatic solar vent, attached to the underside of the lid, controls the interior climate. When the temperature inside the cold frame rises above 85 degrees F, a pressure piston opens the lid several inches so air can circulate. When the temperature drops, the lid closes.

You can build this 6x3-foot cold frame from lengths of weather-treated 1x6 pine boards nailed to 2x2 corner posts. So the whole structure gets as much sun as possible, the hinged polyurethane lid fits over a frame that slopes from 18 inches high in back to only 8 inches in front.

If a cold frame is part of a larger food-growing setup—a greenhouse or outdoor garden, for example—a small, portable unit, such as the one shown *at left,* may be all you need. The cold frame is inexpensive to build, and you can use it to start early-season vegetables, help seedlings make the transition from your greenhouse to an outdoor garden, or cover small plots to keep vegetables producing into fall and early winter.

This cold frame's light weight is the key to its versatility. Make the 3x4-foot frame from pieces of 1x2 redwood lumber, and use clear plastic sheeting to form the walls. To protect plants when the temperature drops, simply roll a plastic cover down over the top.

COLD FRAMES
AND COVER-UPS
(continued)

To shelter tender plants and warm the soil beneath, you can buy double-layered plastic tents, such as those shown *at right*, that extend for an entire row. Their design makes them ruggedly durable yet easy to handle. A layer of black plastic, slit so you can plant seedlings, absorbs heat to warm the soil. A clear plastic layer, suspended by a series of sturdy hoops, protects the plants from the elements. It also has vents along the sides so the vegetables or fruits get enough air. When temperatures go up, you can remove this clear plastic layer. On the other hand, if you're growing heat-loving varieties, such as peppers or tomatoes, be sure to add more protection—a light blanket or sheet—on nights when frost is in the forecast.

Some seeds—parsley, carrots, and celery, for example—germinate slowly. To encourage germination, a cloche can raise the soil temperature and moisture levels in a planting bed. The design shown *at right* does that well and is simple to build. Place panes of glass, in the form of a tent, over the newly planted seeds; hold the glass together with aluminum clips. After the seeds have sprouted, keep the glass tent in place to protect the young plants.

Undercover assignments have always fascinated the French. Around 1900, they devised a way to extend the growing season by raising plants under the protection of a special jar called a *cloche*. Today, a cloche is any transparent structure that is designed to give crops a head start in spring or to prolong the growing season in fall and, depending on the climate, even into winter. Contemporary cloches often cover an entire row of crops.

Grow cold-hardy plants year round in a cloche. You can buy fiber glass cones like those shown *at right* to protect individual plants. These cones are 30 inches wide at the base and have a small hole at the top so air can circulate. As the air within the cone heats, it rises to the top, then condenses on the fiber glass walls. With this kind of protection, you can have fresh spinach, leeks, and other hardy greens while snow still covers the rest of your garden.

If you have many young plants—especially early, cool-season crops—cover entire rows of them with economical cloches like the two shown *at right*. Make them from lengths of clear plastic reinforced with wire netting. Cut the plastic from a roll, bend it into an arch, then anchor the edges to the soil with wire clips. U-shape pieces of a wire coat hanger do the job well.

These plastic sanctuaries do an excellent job of protecting cool-weather crops from late winter frosts. When it's windy, provide extra protection by blocking one end of each cloche with a piece of wood.

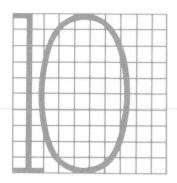

SOLAR
PROJECTS

No one can do much about the weather outside, but with sun-shading devices, movable window and sky-light insulation, and a few modifications to your entryways, you can do a lot to control the effects of weather on your heating and cooling bills. This chapter presents 13 strategies you can employ to keep heat and cold where you want them, along with a couple of other do-it-yourself projects—thermosiphoning air panels and solar water heaters—that can further reduce energy costs.

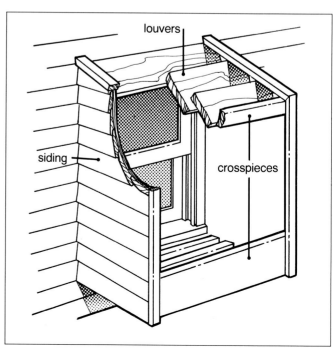

louvers

siding

crosspieces

In hot months, there's really only one way to win the energy-conservation game: Keep the sun out of your house. Rather than try to combat heat already absorbed through your windows, prevent the sun from entering your home in the first place with an exterior sun-shading device. A well-designed sun visor can drastically reduce heat buildup and add new architectural character to your home.

The sun visor shown *opposite* does double duty by also serving as a plant box. As you can see from the shadow in the photograph, the visor shields the windows from the sun, but lets the plants get the light they need.

Concentrate your efforts to provide shading on the sides of your house where the sun is most intense—east, west, or south. In summer, the sun travels in an arc high over your house, at an angle that varies according to your geographic location. Ask your local weather service for the highest angle of summer sun in your area and construct your visor accordingly. Because the angle of the louvers is fixed and the overhang is short, this visor will be most effective on a south-facing window, where it shields your home from overhead sun. Page 136 shows a sun screen that works well on east- or west-facing windows.

To build this visor, first size the unit to fit your window, extending the box about 10 inches below the windowsill. Using galvanized nails, build the basic framework—the top and bottom header pieces and a slatted bottom for stability and drainage. The side panels here are ¾-inch exterior-grade plywood; the remaining structure is redwood lumber and siding. Nail in the louvers and attach the box to the house with screws into the window frame.

Now apply beveled siding to the panels and caulk the joints where the box meets the house. Attach 1x2 trim; finish with paint.

Attaching awnings above windows was a simple and sensible approach usually taken in the days before air conditioning. Since air conditioning has become the rule, however, awnings have become the exception. Yet that extra shading can reduce the heat gain through your windows by approximately 75 percent. You can buy ready-made fabric or aluminum awnings in a variety of styles and colors, or you can build versions that tie in architecturally with your house.

Beyond the initial work and except for occasional maintenance, awnings serve you daily without any additional effort on your part. And like a bump-out visor, awnings face-lift your house as well as control summer heat. Be sure to base the size and tilt of your awnings on the angle at which the sun enters your windows.

To construct the awning pictured *at right,* build a framework of 2x4s, then attach the frame to the house. Cover it with exterior-grade plywood, then attach cedar siding to the plywood with galvanized nails. To tie the awnings in with the rest of the house, paint the exposed framework and plywood on the awning's under side with the same trim paint used elsewhere. Stain the siding to prevent weathering.

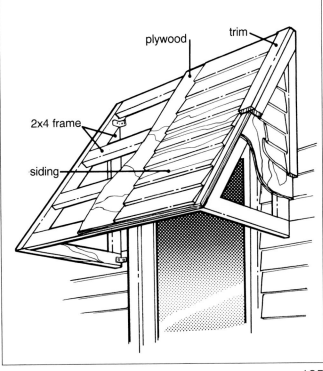

plywood trim

2x4 frame

siding

SUN-SHADING DEVICES
(continued)

Overhangs, awnings, and similar devices help block the intense rays from the sun when it's overhead; but these devices are of little help on the eastern and western sides of a house. As the sun rises and sets, its heat hits these exposures head on. To minimize baking in the early morning or late afternoon, your house needs additional protection.

A louvered sun screen can pick up where an overhang leaves off. Here, a slatted sun screen attached to the roof overhang rests on a raised-bed planter—a bonus you get out of the deal. In this case, the overhang is 4 feet, so with the addition of the sun screen you effectively create a semi-private, sheltered walkway. Also, you can easily tend plants in the raised bed and reach the windows for cleaning and maintenance.

Construction details
You can build the planter box with redwood 2x12s (cedar or treated lumber works well, too); be sure to use galvanized nails so rust stains don't mar the surface later. Add short 4x4 posts for support, then trim the box with a 2x10 cap with mitered corners.

You can use 4x4 redwood, cedar, or pressure-treated posts to frame the fixed louvers. Set the 1x4 louvers 3½ inches apart and at a 30-degree angle, so the view through the windows remains unobscured, yet the area is shaded well. A 1x12 fascia board connects the sun screen to the overhang both physically and visually.

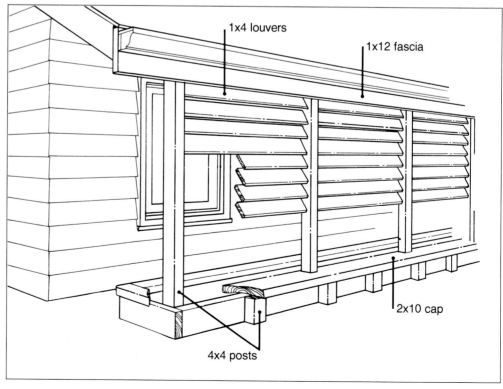

1x4 louvers

1x12 fascia

2x10 cap

4x4 posts

As versatile as it is handsome, the design of this louvered arbor allows it to shade just one window or span the entire side of a house. Best of all, its louvers are adjustable.

The version shown here provides an architectural bonus by unifying different-sized windows and a patio door. For large windows and sliding glass doors, the sunshade should be 54 inches deep; for small windows it need be only 36 inches deep. (If the shade is more than 54 inches deep it requires extra support; if less than 36 inches deep it won't block the sun sufficiently.)

Use 2x8 construction heart redwood to build the frame for the arbor. Cut the ledger 2 inches wider than the window, and screw it into place above the window. Then install the 2x8 side and front pieces and the angled 2x6 braces. Use joist hangers to mount the braces to the side of the house. Cut slots into the side pieces as shown in the photo *above right,* and screw lag bolts loosely into the ends of each louver. Slip the louvers into the slots in the side pieces so the lag bolts act as pivots. Tighten the bolts, and check to make sure each louver swings freely in the slots.

The last step is to attach a nylon cord to operate the louvers. By using a double cord, you can pivot the louvers both forward and backward; and by screwing a 1x2 connecting board to the corners of the louvers and attaching operating cords to the board, you can pivot all the louvers at the same time. Depending on the season and the direction that your window faces, you can pivot the louvers to allow full sun, partial sun, or no sun at all.

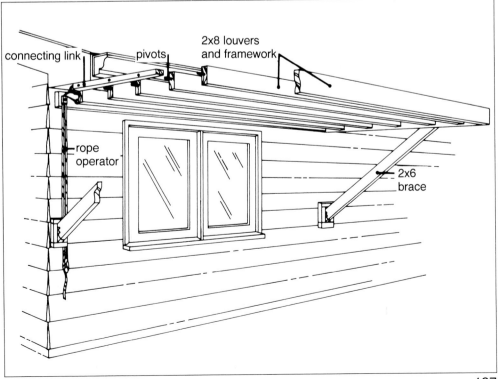

connecting link   pivots   2x8 louvers and framework

rope operator

2x6 brace

DOORWAY
DRAFT STOPPERS

Each time you walk through an exterior door, you have company: air from outside entering or conditioned air from inside leaving. Consider the times you—or the kids or the family pet—come and go, and you'll have a good idea of the drain you place on your cooling or heating system.

To avoid excessive drain, add an air-lock vestibule, a boxed-in area at an entry that traps air pressure between an inner and an outer door. As long as you close one door before opening the other, the inside and outside air won't create a draft that will cause your home to lose its valuable temperature-controlled air. Air-lock entries make special sense for north or northwest entries, or for any exposure if the door opens directly into a main living area. If yours is a region where excessive summer heat gains are a big problem, an air-lock might also make sense on a southern or western exposure.

Of course an exterior air-lock entry must complement your home's architecture and be large enough so you can open one door, step inside, close it, then open the second door. You can build an exterior vestibule more easily on a home with a stoop or other structure to act as a founda-tion; it would cost a good deal more to add one to a home that has no support for the addition. If this is the case at your house, consider an *interior* vestibule, as explained on page 139.

Building out

The entry *below* went on during a face-lifting in which a porch was torn away. The exterior and interior were finished in cedar siding to blend in with the house. To harmonize with the architectural lines above it, the entry roof was slanted, creating an ideal place for a skylight that admits daylight.

To build an exterior vesti-bule, attach 2x4 plates to the old stoop or porch, then frame the walls and roof with con-ventional stud-and-rafter con-struction. Insulation in the walls and a tight-fitting new door will further help conserve energy.

Exterior alternatives

Or consider building a vesti-bule that's all or partially glass. In summer it could also serve as an inviting place for plants. If your home already has an acceptable-looking front porch, you might prefer to simply enclose all or part of it with new sidewalls, perhaps includ-ing storage for coats, muddy boots, and other outdoor gear you'd rather not keep inside the house.

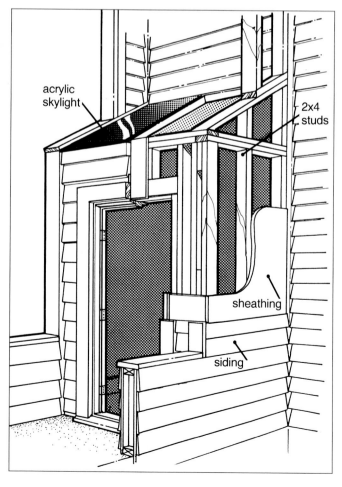

acrylic skylight

2x4 studs

sheathing

siding

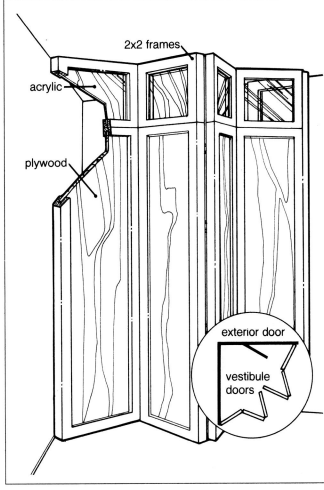

I f you don't want to change the outside appearance of your house or if you don't have space for an exterior air-lock addition, consider building one inside. An interior version will cost only a fraction of its outside counterpart.

Because it needn't stand up to the elements, an interior air-lock can be constructed in a wide variety of ways. The one shown here is essentially a tall, six-panel screen with hinged doors that zigzag to enclose a corner entry. Each panel has a clear acrylic transom up top and papered plywood inset below. Four panels (the two

nearest the walls on each side) are stationary; the two on the inside, which swing to open and close, form the interior "doors."

To build a vestibule like this, use 2x2s for framing members, ½-inch plywood for the bottom sections, and ¼-inch acrylic for the top portions. Construct each panel by cutting dados in the framing members for the plywood and acrylic sheets. (Or, instead of making dados, sandwich the sheets between ½x½-inch quarter round molding.)

Stand the two outside sections at a 45-degree angle to

the walls. With lag screws, anchor the 2x2s to the ceiling, walls, and floor. Weather-strip at the top, bottom, and sides.

Next, attach the second two stationary panels at right angles to the outside panels. Again, weather-strip where adjoining sections meet.

Now you're ready to make the doors and the transoms above them. Install the transoms first, then use butt hinges to hang the doors. Add magnetic catches and a lap-over stop strip along one door edge to seal the crack where the doors meet. Paint or cover the panels with fabric.

Interior alternatives
The advantage of this vestibule is that its triangular shape subtracts a bare minimum of floor space from the room. If you have more space, you could simply build a square or rectangular version. All you need is enough room to step inside and close one door before opening the other. Making the walls all glass or acrylic will minimize its visual bulk, but for economy, you might also choose to opt for all-plywood or conventional stud-and-drywall construction.

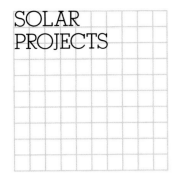

SOLAR PROJECTS

A POP-IN WINDOW SHUTTER

During the day, windows admit the sun's rays into your home, warming it both physically and psychologically. At night, however, their panes work like a sieve and lose precious warmth, degree by degree. At best, a double-paned window creates an insulating factor—that is, resistance to heat loss—of close to R2. With a rigid pop-in panel like the one shown *at left*, however, you can increase the insulating value to R4, greatly reducing the amount of heat that flows out. As a bonus, this decorative panel doubles as a wall hanging by day.

The pop-in shutter is made from semirigid, foil-faced fiber glass, a material also used for ceiling tile. The frame is a U-shape metal channel. Read further for panel construction instructions.

How to make the panel

The panel should fit snugly inside your window frame. Before making any measurements, check the angles of the window corners with a square; if they're out of square, you'll need to make adjustments when you cut the panel. Then make your measurements and subtract ½ inch from each dimension to determine the size to cut the fiber glass board. (Boards come in 4x8- and 4x10-foot sheets.) Make adjustments for any irregularities in the corners.

To make the frame, first put the metal channel against one side of the fiber glass panel

and mark the channel precisely at the corner. Instead of cutting each side to fit, make a V cut at that point, then bend the metal around the fiber glass to form a mitered corner (see illustration, *top right*). Use tin snips or a hacksaw and miter box to make the V cut in the metal channel. Mark, cut, and bend another channel strip to form the other two sides.

For a vapor barrier, cut a sheet of polyethylene 2 to 3 inches larger all around than the fiber glass panel. Lay the polyethylene over the panel's fiber glass (not foil) side, wrapping the sheet around the edges. Coax the fiber glass panel into the metal channel frame; the vapor barrier should remain in place.

Brace the mitered corners of the frame and cover any sharp edges with duct tape. Then wrap adhesive-backed foam weather stripping around the perimeter of the frame; the weather stripping should be as close as possible to the frame edge that will be next to the window pane.

Cover the panel with fabric

So you can remove the fabric for washing, attach it to the panel using nylon self-gripping fasteners. First, with the foil side of the panel facing up, attach 2-inch lengths of self-gripping tape around the frame and at each corner of the panel with epoxy (see illustration, *middle right*). Cut the fabric to fit the panel, adding 2 to 3 inches all around so it will overlap the frame. Iron the fabric and place it on the opposite (polyethylene-covered) side of the panel. Lap the fabric over the panel and temporarily pin it in place. So you'll know where the self-

gripping strips should be, pin them to the fabric while it's in place, lining them up with the strips on the frame. Also, use pins to mark each of the four corners.

Next, sew the corners of the cover. (Just leave the pieces of self-gripping tape pinned to the fabric while you work.) To do this, fold the fabric diagonally with right sides together so the pin marking the corner is on the fold. Sew a one-inch seam at a 45-degree angle to the fold, beginning at the pin marker (see illustration, *bottom right*). Trim the seam. Repeat this step for each corner. Hem the raw edges of the fabric, then sew the self-gripping strips in place on the wrong side of the fabric. Your cover is now ready to place on the panel.

Prepare the panel for hanging

So you can hang the panel on the wall by day, punch a couple of holes directly across from each other in the sides of the frame. Then insert screws in the holes and attach picture wire to them.

Using a double thickness of fabric, sew two 8x1-inch tabs. Then punch holes in the bottom of the frame for attaching the tabs. Tighten a screw through the fabric and into the holes to secure the fabric. Attach a nylon self-gripping dot to each tab pull and to the back of the panel so none of the tabs show when the panel hangs on the wall.

fiber glass board

metal channel

bend at v-cut

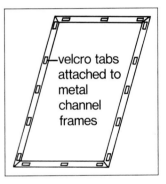

velcro tabs attached to metal channel frames

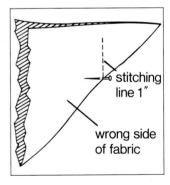

stitching line 1″

wrong side of fabric

141

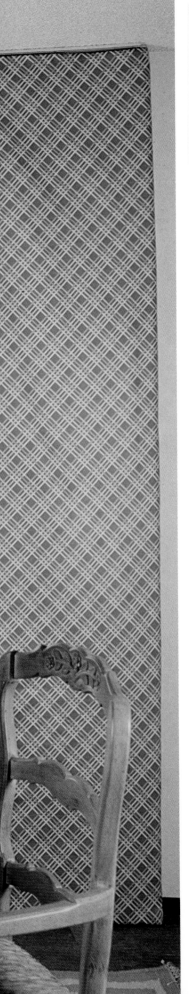

SLIDING PANELS

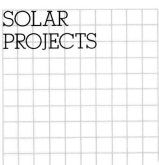

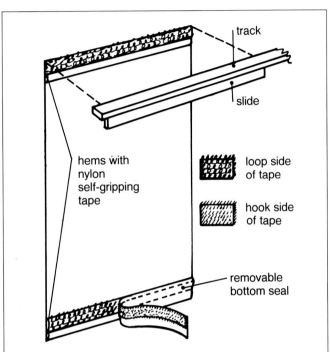

track

slide

hems with
nylon
self-gripping
tape

loop side
of tape

hook side
of tape

removable
bottom seal

You can prevent large expanses of glass or sliding glass doors from wasting energy by covering them with sliding insulating panels such as these. Magnetic tape seals the panels tightly together at night; during the day, they separate and slide neatly behind fixed panels on either side of the doors or window. Edge seal boards, projecting about 2 inches from the wall, meet the panels at 90-degree angles to prevent air leaks.

You'll need cover fabric, commercially made insulative lining, a panel track kit (which includes nylon self-gripping tape and weight bars), and magnetic tape.

First install the track on the ceiling about 2 inches out from the wall. Then mount an L bracket at each end of the track for the edge seal boards. Cut two boards floor-to-ceiling

length and the same width as the space between the track and the wall, and hang from the brackets, as shown in the drawing.

Making the moving panels

Cut the lining for the moving panels ½ inch shorter than the floor-to-track measurement and as wide as the track slides. Finished length of the stationary side panel lining is the same as the floor-to-ceiling measurement. Finished width should be the same as the moving panels plus 1 inch for the thickness of the edge seal board plus the depth of the side return, plus ½ inch.

Cut your cover fabric 3 inches wider and longer than the lining. With right sides facing, pin lining and cover fabric together. Match the side edges and extend the cover fabric over the lining's top and bottom edges by 1½ inches. Stitch side seams ½ inch from

the edges, zigzag along the edges, then turn the panels. To determine placement of magnetic tapes, lay panels on the floor in the positions they'll be in on the track. Mark the location of the tapes so one panel seals to the other when closed. Turn the panels inside out again and add the magnetic strips. (Only one layer of fabric should cover the strips.) To hem, press top edges down ½ inch, then roll them down another inch and press again. Sew a strip of self-gripping tape (the length depends on dimensions of your panels) along the second press line. Then fold the hem down and slip-stitch. Do the same at the bottom, being sure to slip in a weight bar before sewing the hem closed.

Making the stationary panels

Stationary panels should touch the floor after hemming. To make the bottom seals, which are removable for laundering, cut a strip of cover fabric 4½ inches wide and one inch longer than the width of a panel. Fold the fabric lengthwise with right sides together, then stitch ½ inch from the raw edges. Turn, then fold the side edges under ½ inch, press, and stitch. Stitch a strip of self-gripping tape along the seamed edge and attach the seal to the bottom of each panel. Finally, wrap fabric of stationary panels around the edge seal boards. To secure them, sew strips of self-gripping tape to the underside of each panel and staple corresponding strips to the boards.

WINDOW MATS

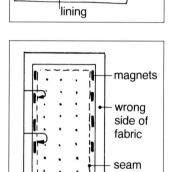

batting

lining

magnets

wrong side of fabric

seam line

Here's an energy-saving window treatment that blends with almost any decorating style. Whether you prefer pleated draperies (as shown here), shirred curtains, slick mini-slat blinds, or even shutters, a window mat like the one shown in use *opposite* lets you keep the treatment you like and still insulate your windows.

The mat, made of layers of insulating material, vapor barrier, and decorative fabric, can be sized to fit any window casing. Depending on your decorating scheme, make the mat a design element in its own right by choosing an attention-getting fabric, or let it be as unobtrusive as possible with a neutral fabric.

At night, the mat seals tightly to the window trim with magnetic tape, which is sewn into the edges of the mat and attached to the corresponding portions of window trim. During the day, the mat pulls off easily and rolls up to become an attractive bolster (or foot warmer) for a sofa or bed, as shown *at right*.

Even if you're a novice sewer you can make this mat. You'll need decorative cover fabric, magnetic tape (available in fabric stores and window specialty shops), grommets and hooks, and—for the mat's insulative lining—drapery lining, two layers of bonded batting, and a vapor barrier, such as the plastic sheeting used for garden mulching.

How to sew it

First, determine the size of the finished mat by measuring the window (including casing and sill), then adding 4 inches to both the height and width. The finished mat should overlap the window by at least 2 inches.

To assemble the insulative lining, layer the following in this order (see illustration *top right*): panels of drapery lining (cut ½ inch longer and wider than the finished mat size) right side down, batting, vapor barrier, and more batting. Baste around the edges, then stitch one inch from all edges.

For the cover, cut your decorative fabric 5 inches wider and longer than the finished mat size. Pin the cover fabric (right side up) to the insulative lining. (The fabric will overlap the insulating layer 2½ inches along all the edges.) Then, baste the layers together, and tack every 4 inches across the entire mat.

Place cut-to-fit strips of magnetic tape along the sides and top of the lining inside the stitch line and along the bottom edges. Then hem the mat by pressing all the edges of the cover fabric under ½ inch, folding the edges over the magnetic tapes, and stitching. (See illustration *lower right*.)

Hanging the mat

To mount the mat, insert a grommet at each end of the top hem. (Grommet kits are available at fabric shops or hardware stores.) Position small screw-in hooks on the window trim to match the positions of the grommets in the mat.

Apply self-sticking magnetic tape around the window to correspond to the magnetic tape strips sewn into the mat itself. (You can paint the strips on the window trim to match the trim without impairing their function.) Hang the mat in place on the hooks and press the edges to seal tightly.

SKYLIGHT
COVER-UPS

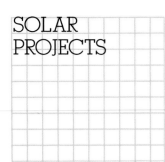

A skylight, no matter how energy efficient, is a hole cut in an otherwise better-insulated ceiling. Corking it with movable insulation helps reduce heat losses, and also offers a way to block out unwanted summer heat.

Here *movable louvers* on the indoor side of a skylight provide the insulation. Each louver is made of rigid foam insulation sandwiched between and glued to pieces of ¼-inch cedar plywood. Aluminum angles, covered with cedar trim, run the long way down each edge to help prevent warping. Weather stripping assures a tight fit.

The louvers pivot on flush bolts normally used to secure the fixed door in a double-door installation, with stops to keep the louvers from pivoting more than 90 degrees. Since they move easily, they're operable manually with a pole.

A *sliding ceiling panel* not only minimizes heat gain or heat loss, but also can add a decorative element to what is an otherwise bland ceiling.

The version shown *above* consists of a frame—twice the size of the skylight—in which a fabric-covered slab of rigid foam can be manipulated by a pair of cords. Pull one cord and the panel slides up to cover the skylight; pull the other and it slides down overtop a second, fixed panel.

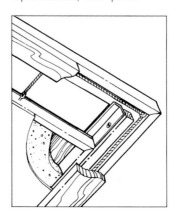

Build the frame first: Each L-shape 1x2 side rail includes a ½x¾-inch nailer strip spaced to create an opening the rope runs through. The panel slides along ⅛x1x1 aluminum angle glued to the side rails.

Now fabricate the panels. For the fixed one, staple fabric to hardboard; for the movable one, frame rigid foam insulation in a weather-stripped frame of 1x1s and cover with fabric. Attach screw eyes to the panel's leading edge.

Assemble the unit by dropping the movable panel into the frame and threading the operating cords through screw-eye guides. Lift the assembly to the ceiling and screw through the nailers to ceiling joists. Screw the fixed panel to the ceiling.

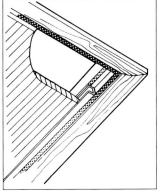

Consider combining both of the ideas shown *opposite* by installing a set of *cord-operated louvers* such as the ones shown *above*. These work much like the ones on window shutters, with a movable center bar hinged to each louver.

To construct each louver, frame a 1-inch-thick piece of rigid foam with 1x¾-inch lumber, cover it with ¼-inch hardboard, and bevel the long edges. Bore holes exactly in the center of each end and glue in ½-inch dowels to serve as pivots. These will fit into holes bored in 1x2 side rails.

If you have an inside frame on your skylight, you're now ready to nail the 1x2s to the skylight frame. If not, first construct one from 1x8s.

Now fit the dowels into the side rails and attach a 1x1 center bar to the louvers' top edges with small hinges. Lift this assembly into the skylight frame and nail the rails to it. Thread the pull cords and weather-strip the edges of the louvers for a snug fit.

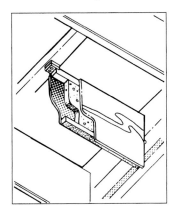

You can create a glare-free skylight (or window) and insulate it with a single effort by installing a *translucent pop-in panel*. Even though this minimizes heat loss and gain, 76 percent of the available outside light still comes through. If you wish, leave the panel in place all the time (often a good idea where excessive heat gain is a primary concern).

The translucent panel is double-walled polypropylene, which is about ¼ inch thick. You can buy it in 2x8-, 3x8-, and 4x8-foot panels and cut it to fit. You may wish to size the

panel so it fits flush inside the skylight frame, and finish it with plastic channel edging. Or overlap the skylight and fasten the panels to the casing with special mounting strips, self-gripping tape, magnets, or sliding tracks.

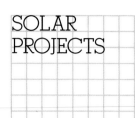

PASSIVE SOLAR
AIR PANELS

Remember those thermo-siphoning air panels shown on page 82? Thermosiphoning air panels—TAPs for short—transfer the heat they collect into a house through air vents cut into the house wall. Warm air enters the house through vents at the top of the wall, and cold air returns to the collector for reheating through vents at the bottom.

TAPs make excellent space heaters. What's more, they're one of the few types of solar collectors simple enough for an average do-it-yourselfer to build. Study the panels shown in the photo *at left* and the drawing *below* and you'll discover how, with some fairly basic carpentry, you too could tap the sun's energy.

Getting started

Begin by determining the number and sizes of panels needed. Mark their locations on the house siding, and check the interior wall to make sure the vents will be unobstructed. Shift the TAP if possible so it lines up with the wall studs as shown in the illustration.

If your home has lap siding, you'll have to cut it away to expose the sheathing under-neath. This gives you an even surface to mount to. If you have plywood or other sheet siding, you don't need to re-move it to install the panels.

Now construct the TAP frame with 2x4s, adding a center mullion if your collector will be two panels wide. Nail rigid foam boards to the back of the frame, and cut and install the seats for the absorber plate and glazing.

Next cut out the top and bottom vent openings in the exterior sheathing and inside wall surface. (Before begin-ning, be sure to turn off the electricity in the part of wall where you'll be working.)

Mounting the unit

Now measure and cut the bot-tom wall bracket. Level and install it, fastening to the band joist, sill, or studs with lag screws. The wall bracket sup-ports most of the weight of the TAP, so be sure it's installed securely.

The next step is to mount the TAP frame to the house. Nail the bottom of the TAP to the wall bracket and attach the top of the frame with angle brackets. Cut vent holes through the insulation that forms the back of the TAP, and cut and install flashing to fit around the vent hole so no wood is exposed.

Now prepare the absorber plate from corrugated alumi-num. Degrease and paint the plate with flat-black, heat-resistant paint. Position the plate onto the absorber seat and nail in place. Then position and install the glazing surface. Trim the exterior of the TAP, and attach flashing at the top of the frame to prevent water seepage onto the wall. Install grills and backdraft dampers over the open vents on the interior wall, and finish the panels to match your house.

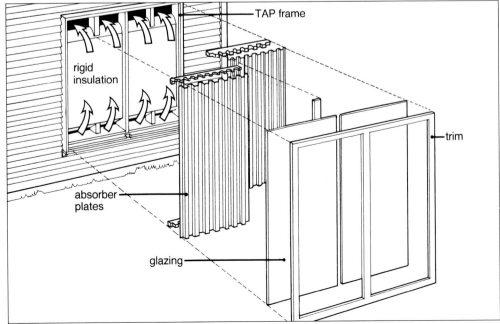

PASSIVE SOLAR WATER HEATERS

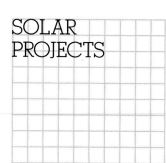

Most do-it-yourself solar water heaters simply preheat water before it's warmed by your regular water heater. And passive heaters—sometimes called "batch" heaters because they heat water in one big batch—work only during the months when there's no danger of freezing; come the cold months, you simply drain the preheat system. Nevertheless, a batch heater can go a long way toward reducing your energy bills—for a cash outlay considerably less than you'd pay for a more sophisticated, commercially made solar water heater.

Batch heaters usually consist of one or two storage tanks in an insulated, glazed box. The 30-gallon heater shown here is one of the easiest systems to build. Construct the box as shown in the illustration, paint or finish it, and insert the plywood "cradles" that hold the tank in place. Lay insulation between the cradles, then nail sheets of aluminum flashing to the top of the cradles to serve as a reflector.

Prepare and plumb the tank as described on page 151. Connect the water lines to your existing hot water system, and cover the top of the box with glazing.

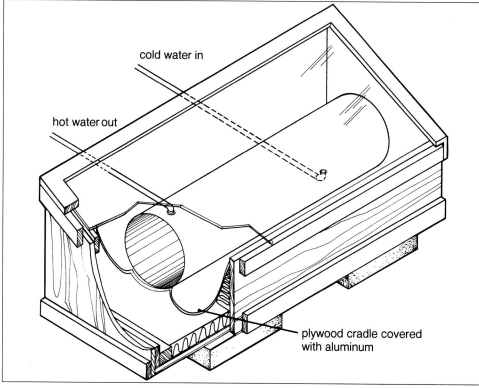

cold water in

hot water out

plywood cradle covered with aluminum

This batch heater is a two-tank, upright-mounted system capable of providing warm water for a family of four. One of the virtues of upright tanks is that they have good thermal stratification; that is, in them hot water tends to rise to the top of the tank and cool water tends to drop to the bottom. This means that water drawn from the top of the tank into the house is always the warmest in the tank.

To build the heater, first construct the stand and the box that holds the water tanks as shown in the illustration. (Boxing in the frame will give the system a more finished look.) Then paint or finish the box and frame to match your house.

Insulate the box with foil-faced, rigid foam insulation. Be sure the reflective foil faces the inside of the box; the foil helps reflect the sun's rays onto the tanks. For greater reflectance, cut two lengths of insulation about 10 inches wide and place them in the corners of the box at a 45-degree angle.

Preparing the tanks
For tanks, try to find a couple of discarded electric water heaters. All you need are the tanks, but test them to make

sure they don't leak. You can also purchase new galvanized pressure tanks. If you buy used water heaters, tear off their outer skins and insulation, and clean the bare tanks with a wire brush or sandpaper. Paint the tanks with flat-black, heat-resistant paint.

Lay the tanks in the box between 2x4s nailed to prevent the tanks from shifting (see photo *at right*). Locate and cut all the holes for the pipes through the box, and plumb the tanks. Make sure there are no leaks, and then strap the tanks into place. Mount the box onto the frame and fasten it securely.

Next, install the inlet supply pipes and connect the batch heater line to your regular water line. Cut off the water supply to your regular heater, and test the batch heater one last time for leaks. Insulate all plumbing lines, wrapping aluminum tape (not duct tape) around the insulation covering the pipes inside the box. The aluminum tape will prevent the insulation from degrading. Have the plumbing inspected if required by local codes.

Finish with glazing
The last step is to cover the box with glazing, using any type of translucent material you wish. The heater shown here is glazed with polyester reinforced with fiber glass; the unit on page 150 is covered with glass. Finish the edges of the box with battens. If you wish, you can also construct shutters to cover the glazing at night. Use foil-faced rigid insulation for the interior panel, and the shutters will serve as reflectors during the day as well.

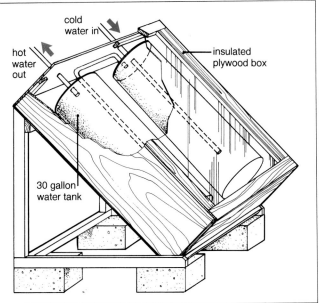

cold water in

hot water out

insulated plywood box

30 gallon water tank

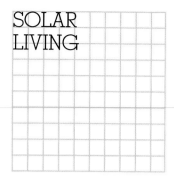

SOLAR LIVING

A GLOSSARY OF SOLAR TERMS

Active solar system. A solar energy system that uses mechanical devices, such as fans and pumps, to distribute collected heat.

Air-to-air heat exchanger. A ventilating device that extracts heat from and exhausts stale household air, then draws in and warms fresh outdoor air.

Air collector. A collector that uses air for heat transfer. A passive solar air collector distributes collected heat via thermosiphoning action.

Batch heater. A passive solar water heater in which the water tanks are enclosed in a glazed, insulated box and placed in the sun to be heated in one big batch.

British thermal unit (BTU). A measurement of heat; the quantity needed to raise the temperature of one pound of water one degree Fahrenheit.

Chimney effect. A means of inducing ventilation by setting up a large enough temperature difference to effect the displacement of warm air by cooler air, often in a thermal chimney. The lighter, warm air rises and is replaced by the cooler air.

Clerestory. A window located high in a wall near the eaves; used for light, heat gain, and often ventilation.

Closed loop system. An active solar system in which the heat transfer liquid (usually a mixture of antifreeze and water) is circulated in a closed loop and at no time is open to the air.

Collection. The gathering of solar heat, usually by passive methods.

Collector. A device that collects solar radiation and converts it to heat; usually refers to active solar collectors.

Conduction. The flow of heat through a material (usually solid) or from one material to another in direct physical contact.

Controls. Devices such as sensors and thermal window coverings that regulate the collection and distribution of heat in a passive solar system.

Convection. Heat transfer caused by the rise of lighter, warm air and the fall of heavier, cool air. In passive solar distribution systems, the convective loop continues as long as the air is rewarmed during the cycle.

Degree-day. A unit of heat measurement equal to the difference between a fixed temperature (usually 65 degrees F) and the average temperature for the day. The total number of degree days for the year indicates the relative severity of a climate.

Direct solar gain. A passive solar heating system in which solar radiation is admitted directly into the living space.

Distribution. The movement of collected heat to the living areas from collectors or storage areas.

Double-glazing. Two layers of glazing with an air space between.

Drainback system. An open-loop hot water system in which the water circulating in the collectors drains back into a storage tank to prevent the collectors from freezing. The water in the system is not the same water used in the home.

Draindown system. An open-loop hot water system in which the water circulating in the collectors is drained by a valve if the collector temperature drops below a certain point. The water heated in the collectors is the same water used in the home.

Earth tube. A tube that draws hot outside air underground, where it is cooled by the earth before entering the house.

Glazing. A translucent or transparent material (such as glass, plastic, or fiber glass-reinforced polyester) that allows light to pass through.

Heat capacity. The number of BTUs required to raise the temperature of one cubic foot of a material one degree Fahrenheit.

Heat exchanger. A device that transfers heat from one fluid to another without mixing the two.

Heat sink. A heat storage medium; thermal mass.

Hybrid solar system. A solar heating system that combines active and passive aspects (usually, a passive solar system that includes a mechanical method of heat distribution).

Indirect solar gain. A type of passive solar heating system in which a heat storage wall (*see* Trombe wall) is placed between the glazing and living space.

Isolated solar gain. A type of passive solar heating system in which heat is collected in one area (usually a sunspace) for use in another.

Insolation. The total amount of solar radiation (direct, diffuse, and reflected) striking a surface, such as a window, exposed to the sky.

Insulation. A material that has a high resistance (measured as R-value) to heat flow; usually used to prevent heat loss.

Kilowatt. A measure of power or heat flow rate; it equals 3,413 BTUs per hour.

Kilowatt hour (kwh). The amount of energy equivalent to one kilowatt of power being used for one hour: 3,413 BTUs.

Liquid collector. A collector that uses a liquid (such as water) for heat transfer.

Magnetic south. The direction south as indicated by a compass.

Movable insulation. A device (such as a thermal window shutter or shade) that reduces heat loss at night or during cloudy periods and permits heat gain in sunny periods; it may also be used to reduce heat gain in summer.

Open-loop system. An active solar domestic hot water system in which water circulates through the collectors. In cold weather, the piping loop in which the water circulates is opened to drain the water from the system, thus preventing freeze-ups.

ACKNOWLEDGMENTS

Passive solar system. A solar energy system that uses natural methods (such as conduction, convection, and radiation) to distribute collected heat. Usually, the structure itself (the house) collects and stores the heat.

Percent possible sunshine. The percentage of the time the sun is shining; usually measured on a monthly basis.

Phase-change materials. Chemical materials (such as certain salts and waxes) that change from solid to liquid as they store heat, and from liquid to solid as they release heat. Phase-change materials have a very high heat-holding capacity.

Photovoltaic cell. A semiconductor device that converts light into electricity. Direct current is produced.

Radiation. The flow of heat, either from the sun or a warm surface, by electromagnetic waves. The means by which heat is released from a thermal mass.

Retrofit. An existing building modified by the addition of some type of solar heating system.

Rock bed. A bin or bed of rocks used to store heat.

Solar fraction. The percentage of a building's yearly heating requirement provided by a solar system.

Storage. A device or medium, such as a phase-change material or a masonry floor, that absorbs collected solar heat and stores it for later use.

Sunspace. A living space that is enclosed with glazing to collect the sun.

Superinsulation. Large amounts of insulation installed in a building to prevent heat loss and therefore decrease heating needs.

Therm. A quantity of heat equal to 100,000 BTUs; approximately 100 cubic feet of natural gas.

Thermal mass. Technically, the total amount of heat storage capability of a passive solar heating system. Often refers to the materials (such as masonry or water) used to store the heat.

Thermal resistance (R-value). The tendency of a material to retard the flow of heat.

Thermogram. An infrared photograph that shows the heat loss of a building

Thermosiphoning. The natural movement of air (or liquid) as it's heated and cooled. Light, warm air rises; heavy, cool air falls.

Trombe wall. A masonry wall, typically 8 to 16 inches thick, darkened and exposed to the sun behind glazing; in a passive solar heating system the wall collects, stores, and distributes heat.

True south. The direction of the sun (or its east to west position) exactly halfway between sunrise and sunset. True south often varies considerably from magnetic south.

Architects, Designers, Builders, and Consultants

The following is a list of architects, designers, builders, and solar systems consultants whose works appear in this book.

Page 7
 Kelly Jordan, ASID
Pages 8-9
 W. Lamar Cheatham III
Pages 12-13
 Robert Young
Page 14
 Ralph F. Jones AIA;
 Paul Pietz, Total
 Environmental Action;
 Thermal Comfort, Inc.
Pages 16-17
 Randy Schwartz, Claude
 Terry and Associates
Page 18
 Solergy Co.
Page 19
 Solarworks Plus
Page 21
 Dave Dussair
Page 22 (top)
 Rob Robinson
Page 22 (bottom)
 Solar Design Associates;
 Builders Collaborative, Inc.
Pages 24-25
 Alan Hanks
Page 47
 Elliott Dudnick
Pages 48-49
 Sibly & Seedorf and
 Associates
Pages 50-51
 Bill Church and
 John Maslen, AIA
Page 54
 Don Pederson

Page 56
 Charles Young;
 Pat Laughman, Armstrong
 World Industries;
 Lewis Homes
Pages 58-59
 Charles Wing, Cornerstone
 Foundation
Pages 60-61
 Weather Energy Systems,
 Inc.; Sandia Dain
Pages 62-63
 Sun Light and Power Co.;
 Gary Gerber; Ed Nold
Pages 64-65
 Edward C. Collins II, AIA
Pages 66-67
 Robert Skelton and
 William Moorhouse;
 Architects Three;
 Betty Amacker
Pages 68-69
 John Hueser; Shirley
 Darrow, Internationale
 Kitchentechnique, Ltd.
Pages 70-71
 Jim Jennings, Jennings and
 Stout
Pages 72-73
 David Piches

(continued)

ACKNOWLEDGMENTS
(continued)

Architects, Designers, Builders, and Consultants
(continued)

Pages 74-75
Finn Jorgenson;
James Wintersteen
Pages 76-77
John Whitaker
Pages 78-79
Peter J. Pfister, AIA
Pages 80-81
Johnson Olney Associates,
Inc.; Norman Saunders
Page 83
Photic Corp.
Page 84
Solahart
Page 85
Solar Components Corp.
Pages 86-87
Solaron Corp.
Page 88
Solar Alternatives, Inc.
Page 89
Solarworks Plus
Pages 90-91
Landon-Landon &
Associates
Pages 92-93
McMillan Development Co.
Inc.
Pages 100-101
Green Meadows, Ltd.;
Janet Woodruff, Interior
Artistic Design
Pages 102-103
Susan Nichols
Pages 104-105
Dale R. Leyse; Jenny Fitch

Pages 106-107
Bridgie Stokes, Natural
Sonshine
Page 108
Green Meadows, Ltd.;
Rothchild Construction Co.
Page 109
James Schoenfelder, AIA
Page 110
Charles Stinson
Page 111
Stacy L. Strand
Page 113
Richard E. Dobroth;
Peg Dobroth
Page 114
Fisher, Friedman Associates;
Sandra Banks
Pages 116-117
Tanya Berger-Olsen
Page 118
James Plumb, AIA;
Joan Yates
Page 119 (top)
Paintridge Design Inc.;
Barbara Schults
Pages 120-121
Robert E. Dittmer
Pages 122-123
Ron Smolowitz
Pages 124-125
Freeman and Barbara
Chase
Page 130 (bottom), 133 (top)
Leandre Poisson, Solar
Survival

Page 134
The Design Concern
Page 135
John M. Vincent
Page 136
William Dong/Tandem
Page 137
California Redwood
Association
Page 138
Miller/Morris; Urban
Resources Construction
Page 139
The Design Concern
Page 140
Stephanie Gibson
Pages 142-143
Interior Marketing Concepts;
Judy Tretheway
Pages 144-145
Judy Tretheway
Page 146 (left)
John Hueser
Pages 146 (right), 147 (left)
The Design Concern
Pages 148-149, 150
Total Environmental Action
Foundation, Inc.
Page 151
Jeff Tiller, Rick Ruggles,
Mary Witt, Georgia Solar
Coalition

Special thanks
We'd also like to thank the
following for their technical
assistance in writing and
producing this book.

Duro-Test Corporation
General Electric Company
Inframetrics, Inc.
Iowa State University Extension
Office
Solar Energy Research
Institute

Photographers and Illustrators
We extend our thanks to the
following photographers and
illustrators whose creative
talents and technical skills
contributed much to this book.

Art Factory
Ann Bingham
Ernie Braun
Jim Buckels
Bob Calmer
Ross Chapple
Mike Dieter
Jim Downing
Feliciano
D. Randolph Foulds
George de Gennaro Studios
Gorchev & Gorchev
Karlis Grants
Bob Harr and Jim Hedrich,
Hedrich-Blessing
Bill Helms
Hopkins Associates
Pete Krumhardt
Scott Little
Fred Lyon
Marine Arts
Maris/Semel
E. Alan McGee
Tim Street-Porter
Ozzie Sweet
Ted Vaughn
Jessie Walker
Sandra Williams

WHERE TO GO FOR MORE INFORMATION

BETTER HOMES AND GARDENS® BOOKS

Want to learn more about decorating, remodeling, or maintaining your home? These Better Homes and Gardens® books can help.

Better Homes and Gardens®
NEW DECORATING BOOK
How to translate ideas into workable solutions for every room in your home. Choosing a style; furniture arrangements; windows, walls, and ceilings; floors; lighting; and accessories. 433 color photos, 76 how-to illustrations, 432 pages.

Better Homes and Gardens®
COMPLETE GUIDE TO HOME REPAIR,
MAINTENANCE, & IMPROVEMENT
Inside your home, outside your home, your home's systems, basics you should know. Anatomy and step-by-step drawings illustrate components, tools, techniques, and finishes. 515 how-to techniques; 75 charts; 2,734 illustrations; 552 pages.

Better Homes and Gardens®
STEP-BY-STEP
CABINETS AND SHELVES
Materials and hardware, planning guidelines, the ABCs of cabinet construction, cutting and joining techniques, project potpourri. 155 illustrations, 96 pages.

Better Homes and Gardens®
STEP-BY-STEP
BASIC PLUMBING
Getting to know your system, solving plumbing problems, making plumbing improvements, plumbing basics and procedures. 42 projects, 200 illustrations, 96 pages.

Better Homes and Gardens®
STEP-BY-STEP
BASIC WIRING
Getting to know your system, solving electrical problems, making electrical improvements, electrical basics and procedures. 22 projects, 286 illustrations, 96 pages.

Better Homes and Gardens®
STEP-BY-STEP
BASIC CARPENTRY
Setting up shop, choosing tools and building materials, mastering construction techniques, building boxes, hanging shelves, framing walls, installing drywall and paneling. 10 projects, 191 illustrations, 96 pages.

Better Homes and Gardens®
STEP-BY-STEP
MASONRY & CONCRETE
Choosing tools and materials; planning masonry projects; working with concrete; working with brick, block, and stone; special-effect projects. 10 projects, 200 drawings, 96 pages.

Better Homes and Gardens®
STEP-BY-STEP
HOUSEHOLD REPAIRS
Basic tools for repair jobs, repairing walls and ceilings, floors and stairs, windows, doors, electrical and plumbing items. 200 illustrations, 96 pages.

NATIONAL SOLAR ORGANIZATIONS

These organizations can provide more information about solar energy and other renewable resources.

Conservation and Renewable Energy Inquiry and Referral Service
P.O. Box 8900
Silver Spring, MD 20907
(800) 462-4983 in Pennsylvania
(800) 233-3071 in Alaska and Hawaii
(800) 523-2929 in all other states, the Virgin Islands, and Puerto Rico

Community Services Administration Energy
   Conservation Program
200 Nineteenth Street NW
Washington DC 20506
(202) 655-4000

National Center for Appropriate Technology
P.O. Box 3838
Butte, MT 59701
(406) 494-4577

Center for Renewable Resources
1001 Connecticut Avenue NW, Suite 510
Washington, DC 20036
(202) 466-6880

Institute for Local Self-Reliance
1717 18th Street NW
Washington, DC 20009
(202) 232-4108

National Association of Home Builders
15th and M Streets NW
Washington, DC 20005
(202) 452-0271

Solar Energy Research Institute
1536 Cole Boulevard
Golden, CO 80401
(303) 231-1192

Solar Energy Industries Association
1001 Connecticut Avenue NW, Suite 800
Washington, DC 20036
(202) 293-2981

(continued)

WHERE TO GO FOR MORE INFORMATION
(continued)

STATE ENERGY OFFICES

In addition to the offices listed here, many university extension services provide solar energy information and assistance.

Alabama
Alabama Department of Energy
25 Washington Avenue, 4th Floor
Montgomery, AL 36130

Alaska
Alaska Energy Office/Division of Energy and Power Development
Frontier Building, 7th Floor
360l C. Street
Anchorage, AK 99503

Arizona
Arizona Energy Programs
Capitol Tower
1700 West Washington Street, 5th Floor
Phoenix, AZ 85007

Arkansas
Arkansas Energy Office
No. 1 State Capitol Mall
Little Rock, AR 72201

California
California Energy Commission
1111 Howe Avenue, MS-10
Sacramento, CA 95825

Colorado
Colorado Office of Energy Conservation
112 East 14th Avenue
Denver, CO 80203

Connecticut
Office of Policy and Management, Energy Division
80 Washington Street
Hartford, CT 06106

Delaware
Division of Facilities Management, Energy Office
P.O. Box 1401/Margaret O'Neil Building
Federal Street
Dover, DE 19901

District of Columbia
District of Columbia Energy Office
421 Eighth Street
Washington, DC 20004

Florida
Governor's Energy Office
301 Bryant Building
Tallahassee, FL 32301

Georgia
Georgia Office of Energy Resources
270 Washington Street SW, Room 615
Atlanta, GA 30334

Hawaii
Department of Planning and Economic Development
Energy Division
P.O. Box 2359
Honolulu, HI 96804

Idaho
Energy Bureau, Resources Analysis Division
State House Mail
450 W. State Street
Boise, ID 83720

Illinois
Department of Energy and Natural Resources
325 West Adams Street, Room 300
Springfield, IL 62706

Indiana
Indiana Energy Office
440 N. Meridian Street
Indianapolis, IN 46204

Iowa
Iowa Energy Policy Council
Capitol Complex, Lucas Building
Des Moines, IA 50319

Kansas
Kansas Energy Office
503 Kansas Avenue, Room 212
Topeka, KS 66603

Kentucky
Kentucky Department of Energy
P.O. Box 11888
Lexington, KY 40578-1916

Louisiana
Department of Natural Resources
Division of Research and Development
P.O. Box 44156
Baton Rouge, LA 70804

Maine
Maine Office of Energy Resources
State House, Station No. 53
Augusta, ME 04333

Maryland
Maryland Energy Office
301 W. Preston Street, Suite 903
Baltimore, MD 21201

Massachusetts
Executive Office of Energy Resources
100 Cambridge Street, Room 1500
Boston, MA 02202

Michigan
Energy Administration/Michigan Department of Commerce
P.O. Box 30228
Lansing, MI 48909

Minnesota
Department of Energy, Planning and Development
980 American Center Building
150 East Kellogg Boulevard
St. Paul, MN 55101

Mississippi
Mississippi Department of Transportation and Energy
Watkins Building
510 George Street, Suite 3000
Jackson, MS 39202

Missouri
Division of Energy Programs/Department of Natural Resources
P.O. Box 176
1014 Madison
Jefferson City, MO 65102

Montana
Energy Division
Department of Natural Resources and Conservation
32 South Ewing Street
Helena, MT 59620

Nebraska
Nebraska State Energy Office
P.O. Box 95085
301 S. Centennial Mall, 4th Floor
Lincoln, NE 68509

Nevada
Nevada Department of Energy
400 West King Street, Suite 106
Carson City, NV 89710

New Hampshire
Governor's Energy Office
State House Annex, Room 22
Concord, NH 03301

New Jersey
New Jersey Department of Energy
101 Commerce Street
Newark, NJ 07102

New Mexico
New Mexico Department of Energy and Minerals
525 Camino de los Marquez
Santa Fe, NM 87501

New York
New York State Energy Office
2 Rockefeller Plaza, 10th Floor
Albany, NY 12223

North Carolina
North Carolina Energy Division/Department of Commerce
P.O. Box 25249
Raleigh, NC 25249

North Dakota
North Dakota Energy Office
State Capitol, 17th Floor
Bismarck, ND 58505

Ohio
Ohio Department of Energy
State Office Tower, 34th Floor
30 East Broad Street
Columbus, OH 43215

Oklahoma
Oklahoma Department of Energy
4400 N. Lincoln Boulevard, Suite 252
Oklahoma City, OK 73105

Oregon
Department of Energy
Labor and Industries Building, Room 102
Salem, OR 97310

Pennsylvania
Governor's Energy Council
300 North Second Street
Commerce Building, 11th Floor
Harrisburg, PA 17105

Rhode Island
Governor's Energy Office
80 Dean Street
Providence, RI 02903

South Carolina
Governor's Division of Energy Resources
SCN Center, 4th Floor
1122 Lady Street
Columbia, SC 29201

South Dakota
Office of Energy Policy
State Capitol
Pierre, SD 57501

Tennessee
Energy Authority
226 Capitol Boulevard, Suite 707
Nashville, TN 37219

Texas
Texas Energy and Natural Resources Advisory Council
200 East 18th Street, Suite 513
Austin, TX 78701

Utah
Utah Energy Office
3266 State Office Building
State Capitol Complex
Salt Lake City, UT 84114

Vermont
Vermont State Energy Office
State Office Building
Montpelier, VT 05602

Virginia
Virginia Office of Emergency and Energy Services
310 Turner Road
Richmond, VA 23225

Washington
Washington State Energy Office
400 E. Union Avenue, 1st Floor
Olympia, WA 98504

West Virginia
West Virginia Fuel and Energy Division
1426 Kanawaha Boulevard East
Charleston, WV 25301

Wisconsin
Wisconsin Division of State Energy/Department of Administration
101 S. Webster, 8th Floor
P.O. Box 7868, Madison, WI 53707

Wyoming
Wyoming Energy Conservation Office
Capitol Hill Office Building
25th and Pioneer
Cheyenne, WY 82002